ISBN 978-1-334-02906-6
PIBN 10559486

1 MONTH OF
FREE
READING

at
www.ForgottenBooks.com

By purchasing this book you are eligible for one month membership to ForgottenBooks.com, giving you unlimited access to our entire collection of over 1,000,000 titles via our web site and mobile apps.

To claim your free month visit:
www.forgottenbooks.com/free559486

English
Français
Deutsche
Italiano
Español
Português

www.forgottenbooks.com

Mythology Photography **Fiction**
Fishing Christianity **Art** Cooking
Essays Buddhism Freemasonry
Medicine **Biology** Music **Ancient
Egypt** Evolution Carpentry Physics
Dance Geology **Mathematics** Fitness
Shakespeare **Folklore** Yoga Marketing
Confidence Immortality Biographies
Poetry **Psychology** Witchcraft
Electronics Chemistry History **Law**
Accounting **Philosophy** Anthropology
Alchemy Drama Quantum Mechanics
Atheism Sexual Health **Ancient History**
Entrepreneurship Languages Sport
Paleontology Needlework Islam
Metaphysics Investment Archaeology
Parenting Statistics Criminology
Motivational

INITIATION
THE PERFECTING OF MAN

BY

ANNIE BESANT

President of the Theosophical Society

THE THEOSOPHICAL PRESS
826 Oakdale Avenue
CHICAGO

FOREWORD

THERE is nothing new in these lectures, but only old truths retold. But the truths are of such vivid and perennial interest that, though old, they are never stale, and, though well known, there is always something to say which seems to throw on them new light and new charm. For they touch the deepest recesses of our being, and bring the breath of heaven into the lower life of earth.

Constantly immersed as are most in the affairs of daily life, they are apt to lost sight of "the things which belong to their peace," and so any call to "lift up their eyes unto the hills" is welcomed by the earnest and the aspiring. The eternal verities are always restful, as is the view of snowy peaks to those toiling along the dusty roads of valleys far below.

May these reminders of the ancient facts of discipleship and Masterhood nerve some to effort, encourage others to perseverance. May they help some to realize the possibility of obeying the command: "Be ye therefore perfect, even as your Father in heaven is perfect."

ANNIE BESANT.

PREFACE TO AMERICAN EDITION

A new school of thought is arising to challenge long-accepted views of life. Its keynote may be said to be "evolutionary creation." It is an exposition of the phenomena that surrounds us in terms that are both scientific and idealistic. It offers an explanation of life, of the origin of our fragment of the universe, of hidden and mysterious natural laws, of the nature and destiny of man, that appeals with moving force to the logical mind. This school of thought is at the same time both iconoclastic and constructive, for it is sweeping away old dogmas that are no longer tenable in the light of rapidly developing modern science, while it is building a substantial structure of facts beneath the age-long dream of immortality.

The literature that is growing out of ideas which are so revolutionary in the intellectual realm and yet are so welcome to a world groping through the fogs of materialism, is receiving a warm welcome in other lands, and it should be better known here.

THE PUBLISHERS.

CONTENTS

INITIATION
THE PERFECTING OF MAN

THE MAN OF THE WORLD

HIS FIRST STEPS

THERE is a Path which leads to that which is known as Initiation, and through Initiation to the Perfecting of Man; a Path which is recognized in all the great religions, and the chief features of which are described in similar terms in every one of the great faiths of the world. You may read of it in the Roman Catholic teachings as divided into three parts: (1) The Path of Purification or Purgation; (2) the Path of Illumination; and (3) the Path of Union with Divinity. You find it among the Mussulmans in the Sufi— the mystic—teachings of Islam, where it is known under the names of the Way, the Truth and the Life. You find it further eastward still in the great faith of Buddhism, divided into subdivisions, though these can be classified under the broader outline. It is similarly divided in Hinduism; for in both those great religions, in which the study of psychology, of the human mind and the human constitution, has played so great a part, you find a more definite subdivision.[1]

But really it matters not to which faith you turn; it matters not which particular set of names you choose as best attracting or expressing your own ideas; the Path is but one; its divisions are always the same; from time immemorial that Path has stretched from the life of the world to the life of the Divine. Through thousands upon thousands of years some of our human race have trodden it; for thousands and thousands of years which are yet unborn, some of our race shall tread it to the end of our earth story, to the conclusion of this special cycle of human time.

It is the Path which, stage by stage, enables man to fulfil the command of the Christ: "Be ye therefore perfect, even as your Father which is in heaven is perfect." It is the Path whereof that same great Teacher declared: "Strait is the gate and narrow is the way that leadeth unto life, and few there be that find it." I know that in later days, when most men had forgotten the existence

---

[1] The Path of Purification is the Probationary Path, on which certain qualifications must be developed; the Path of Illumination is the Path of Holiness, subdivided into four stages, each of which is entered by a special Initiation, symbolized among Christians as the Birth, Baptism, Transfiguration, and Passion of Christ; the Path of Union is the attainment of Masterhood, Liberation, Final Salvation.

of the Path, they changed those true words
into words that are utterly false, that make
the gate and the way narrow that lead unto
a heavenly life, and broad and wide the way
that leadeth to an everlasting condemnation;
but that is a distortion of the occult teaching.
It is a twisting of the words of the Christ, for
surely He, Whom His followers call the Saviour of the world, could never have declared
that only few should be the ranks of the saved,
practically numberless the crowds of the lost.
In dealing with the Path we are not in those
regions of exoteric faith which speak of
heaven and hell. The life to which the Path
leads the pilgrim is not the life of the passing
joys of heaven; it is that life spoken of in
the fourth gospel, where it is written: "The
knowledge of God is eternal life"—life which
is not counted by endless ages, but which
means a change in the attitude of the man;
which means not time, but a life that is beyond time; which is not counted by the rising
and setting of suns, even though those dawns
and sunsets were in an immortal life; but
which means that perfect serenity, that unity
with God, in which time is only a passing incident of existence, and an ever-present reality is understood as the true life of the Spirit.

And so the Path that we are to study
through the coming Sundays, through these
brief and poor descriptions of what that Path
may mean to man, is the short though diffi-

cult way by which man evolves more rapidly than in the ordinary course of human and natural evolution; it is the Path by which, to use a simile often used, instead of going round and round the mountain by an ever-climbing spiral, man climbs straight up the mountain-side regardless of cliff and precipice, regard-less of gulf and chasm, knowing there is noth-ing that can stop the Eternal Spirit, and that no obstacle is stronger than the strength that is omnipotence, because it has its source in Omnipotence itself.

Such is the Path, then, that you and I are to try to study, not for the mere interest of what is indeed a fascinating and enthralling subject, but rather, at least on the part of the speaker and I hope on the part of some at least of the hearers, a study that is meant to change the life, a study that gives birth to a determination to tread the Path, to know it not only theoretically but by a practical real-ization, and to understand something of those hidden Mysteries by which man, ever poten-tially divine, realizes his inner Divinity and becomes perfect, rising above and beyond hu-manity.

Such is the scope, then, of our study, and in order that the study may be practical, we must assume, at least for the time, the ex-istence of certain great facts in Nature. I do not mean that our man of the world, in tak-ing his first step towards the Path, need either know or recognize these facts. Facts in Nature do not change either with our believing or non-believing. Facts of Nature remain facts whether we know them or not, and since we are here in the realm of Nature, and under the order of law, the knowledge of the facts and the knowledge of the law are not essential for the steps which lead man to the Path. It is enough that the facts are there, and that the man unconsciously is allowing those facts to influence his inner and his outer life. It is enough that the laws exist, although the man may not know of their existence. Sunshine does not cease to warm you because you may not know anything of the constitution of the sun. Fire does not cease to burn you, because, unknowing its fierceness, you thrust your hand into the flame. It is the security of human life and human progress that the laws of nature are ever working and carrying us on with them, whether we know of them or not. But if we know them, we gain a great advantage. If we know them, we can co-operate with them as we cannot co-operate as long as we are in the darkness of ignorance. If we know the facts we can utilize them, as we cannot utilize them when we know not they are there. To know is the difference between walking in the darkness and in the light, and to understand the laws of Nature is to gain the power of quickening our evolution by utilizing every law that hastens our growth, by avoiding the working of those that would retard and delay.

Now, one of the great facts which underlie the whole possibility of a Path of Human Perfecting, that I must take for granted throughout the lectures—for to deal with it as a matter for argument would lead us far away from our subject—one of the fundamental facts in Nature, is the fact of reincarnation. That means the gradual growth of man through many lives, through many experiences of the physical world, of the intermediate world, and also of the world called heaven. Evolution would be too short to enable a man to grow from imperfection to perfection, unless he had many opportunities, a long, long road to lead him upward. And our man of the world who will take the first steps, who is ready to take them, must have behind him a long, long course of human evolution, in which he has learned to choose the good and to reject the evil, in which his mind has been evolved and trained, his character has been built up, from the ignorance and non-moral state of the savage to the point where the civilized man is standing to-day. The fact of reincarnation, then, is taken for granted, for not one of us could possibly tread the whole of that long course, could reach divine perfection, in the limits of a single life. But our man of the world need not know of reincarnation. He knows it in his spiritual memory, although his physical brain may not yet have recognized it, and his past, which is a fact, will push him onwards until Spirit and brain are in fuller communication, and that which is known to the man himself becomes known in the concrete mind.

The next great fact, necessary and taken for granted, may be put into a single phrase of your own Scriptures: "Whatsoever a man soweth that shall he also reap." It is the law of causation, the law of action and reaction, by which Nature brings inevitably to the man the results of that which he has thought, which he has desired, which he has done.

Next, the facts are that there is a Path and that men have trodden it before us; that the swifter evolution is possible; that the laws of it may be known, the conditions of it understood, the stages of it be trodden; and that at the end of that Path there are standing Those Who once were men of the world, but now are the Guardians of the world, the Elder Brethren of our race, the Teachers and the Prophets of the past, stretching upwards in ranks of ever-more dazzling light from the ending of the Path for man to the highest Ruler of the world in which we live. Poor would be our hope if none before us had trodden the Way, if none had walked upon the Path. But They

Who in the past have come as Teachers have in an earlier past accomplished this mighty pilgrimage. Those Whom to-day we honor as Masters exist in touch with our world that They may take pupils, and guide them in the treading of the Path.

These are the great facts in Nature, existing, whether recognized or not, on which the possibility of treading the Path depends: Reincarnation, the law of Karma, the fact of the Path, the Existence of the Teachers. Those are the four facts I must take for granted—not saying that they may not be shown to be true by argument one after the other, but for the purposes of this course taking them for granted—because without each of them the very lectures themselves would be impossible.

What steps, then, is our man of the world to take, or what steps is he taking, if he is really approaching the entrance to the beginning of the Path?

I have said that he need not know the four great truths I have mentioned, he need not understand them or recognize them. That is part of the hopeful side of the subject, that there may be—nay, there will be—many among you who do not yet know the truth of these things, but yet, in the course of evolution, are treading onwards towards the entrance to the Path. And though in time to come you will know more fully, though unconsciously you are evolving, none the less

the evolution is a fact. And what I want to
do this morning is to show you those steps,
that you may be able to consider your own
lives and judge whereabout you stand; that
you may be able to decide, each for himself,
whether or not his face is turned in the direction of the Path; for there are many among
you who are going in the direction, albeit you
know it not, while there are some who, having studied and understood, are deliberately
turning their faces in that direction. To turn
your evolution from being unconscious into
being conscious, to enable you to understand
yourselves, and where you are, that is the
purpose of the first of these lectures; so that
those amongst you who believe in the Path
may know how to live, and that those who,
unknowingly, are approaching it may, perchance, realize the happiness of their lot.

The first step of all, absolutely necessary,
without which no approach is possible, by
which achievement ever comes within reach
of realization, may be summed up in four
brief words: the Service of Man.

There is the first condition, the *sine qua
non*. For the selfish no such advance is possible; for the unselfish such advance is certain. And in whatever life the man begins to
think more of the common good than of his
own individual gain, whether it be in the
service of the town, of the community, of the
nation, of the wider joinings of nations to-

gether, right up to the service of humanity itself, every one of those is a step towards the Path, and is preparing the man to set his feet thereon. And there is no distinction here between the kinds of service, provided they are unselfish, strenuous, moved by the ideal to help and serve. It may be purely intellectual —the work of the writer and the author, trying to spread among others the knowledge he has found, in order that the world may be a little wiser, a little more understanding, because that man has lived and written. It may be along the service of Art, wherein the musician, the painter, the sculptor, the architect, puts before himself the ideal of making the world a little fairer and more beautiful, life a little more sweet, more full of grace and culture for humankind. It may be along the way of Social Service, where the man, moved by sympathy for the poor, the suffering, pours out his life in the work of helping, tries to alter the constitution of Society where it needs amendment, tries to change the environment where the environment of the past, useful in the past, has become an anachronism, and is preventing the better progress that humankind should to-day environment. It may be along the way of Political Work, where the life of a nation, internal and external, is the object of service. It may be along the way of Healing, where the doctor tries to bring health in the place of disease, and to make conditions good for the body, in order that the body may be healthier and longer-lived than otherwise it would be. I cannot give you one by one the numerous divisions of the Way of Service. Anything that is of value to human life is included on that way. Choose then what way you will, because of your capacities and your opportunities; it matters not as regards the treading of the first steps. Commerce, industry, anything of use to man, production, distribution; they all come within Service for man and supply man's necessities.

But you will say that everyone is engaged in one or other of the things I have mentioned, or in similar avocations in life. That is true, because the way to the Path is set in human life, and there is nothing necessary for the growth and evolution of that life which may not be made a step towards the Path. But the difference lies in the conditions of the work. Truly, men follow all these ways and many more; they produce, they distribute, they take part in industry or commerce, they are writers, artists, politicians, social reformers, doctors, what you will; but with what object, and moved by what motive? There lies the difference between the man who is on the ordinary road of evolution, growing by his work or his study, and the man who, while growing, is growing with the object of Service of lifting the world a little higher and not only of earning his livelihood therein. I am not speaking with any idea of looking down upon, or with contempt for, those who are merely walking in the ways of the world with the ordinary worldly objects. That is a part, and a necessary part, of evolution. How should man evolve his mind, how should man train his emotions, how should man develop even physically, unless he considers the ways of the world, and makes efforts to succeed therein? It is well that men should work for the fruit of action, well that men should struggle in order to succeed, well that men should be ambitious, should grasp after power and place, after fame, honor and success. Toys! Yes, they are toys; but they are the toys by which the children learn to walk, the prizes in life's school by which the boys are stimulated to exertion, the crowns in the struggle of life by which strength and energy and future possibilities are developed. Do not despise the common world of men, in which men are striving and struggling, making many an error and many a blunder, committing many a sin and even a crime, for all these are lessons in life's school, all these are stages through which every man must pass. As the fierce struggle in the world of the brute develops strength and cunning and the power to guard the life, so do the fierce struggles among men develop the power of the will, the power of the mind, the power of the emotions, even the power of muscle and of nerve. In a world which springs from infinite Wisdom and infinite Love, there is no lesson in life that has not its purpose, and in all the prizes of the world—call them from the higher standpoint toys as you may—in all the fruits of action which in the higher life you are bidden to renounce and to cast aside; in every one of these God is hiding, in every one of them His attractiveness is the only power that allures, and, though they break into pieces when you have grasped them, although ambition turns to ashes when it is satisfied, although wealth becomes a burden when it is gathered, although pleasure becomes satiety after it has filled the cup of delight; still the breaking is another lesson, the lesson that you may remember was exquisitely put by the Christian poet, George Herbert:

> When God at first made man,
> Having a glass of blessings standing by;
> "Let us (said He) pour on him all we can;
> Let the world's riches, which dispersed lie,
> Contract into a span."
>
> So strength first made a way;
> Then beauty flowed, then wisdom, honor, pleasure.
> When almost all was out, God made a stay,
> Perceiving that alone of all his treasure,
> Rest, in the bottom, lay.
>
> "For if I should (said He)
> Bestow this jewel also on my creature,
> He would adore my gifts instead of me,
> And rest in nature, not the God of nature;
> So both should losers be.

"Yet let him keep the rest;
But keep them with repining restlessness;
Let him be rich and weary, that, at least,
If goodness lead him not, yet weariness
  May toss him to my breast."

There is the great truth of at once the value and the worthlessness of human life: valuable, because it brings out the faculties without which no progress is possible; worthless, because everything breaks into pieces, and leaves the hands empty till at last they grasp the feet of God.

There then is the worth of the ordinary life, and our man of the world has begun to realize that not in seeking pleasure, wealth, and honor for himself can permanent joy be found; but in the service of his fellow-men, in the helping of the miserable, the teaching of the ignorant, the uplifting of the oppressed, the lightening of the sorrow of the poor. And many there are among you to-day who are well off and comfortable, whose hearts are heavy for the sorrow of the world, and who cannot rest in your comfort, in your luxury, while others are starving, miserable, crushed under the burden of life. Oh! the waking of the social conscience amongst us, the recognition of social duty, of social responsibility, is the noblest sign of the evolution of man, a proof of the coming of a new Race that shall have sympathy instead of indifference, co-operation instead of competition, as its rule

in the outer life of man. And as that spreads
and grows, more and more men of the world
will tread these early steps. But it must be
strenuous: not the passing feeling of compassion that makes you out of your superfluity
give what you never miss to some good cause
or some unhappy family; not the throwing
aside of some luxuries you have in order that
others may have more of the necessaries of
life. Much more than that is demanded from
you, O you who would tread towards the entrance to the Path. You must give yourself,
and not only what you possess—and in that
there is an immensity of difference. You must
feel the sorrow of others as you feel your own
pain; you must feel the grief of others as you
feel the piercing of your own heart. It must
come to you as an intolerable goad to action,
that presses you along the Way of Service,
which you cannot deny nor resist. You find
people amongst you like that, people who cannot rest. It is not making sacrifices. That
lies behind them. The things the world calls
sacrifices are their delights; they joy to give
themselves; it is only a sacrifice in the sense
that the Life-Spirit is ever flowing out to others; but that is joy and not sorrow, delight
and not pain, involuntary, almost a necessity
of life. And where you see that passion of
Service, where you see that willingness to
give everything up that others may be happier, where you see people ever thinking what

they can do to help, whom they can find to serve, who there is near them to whom they can render help—it may be within the circle of the family or in the larger circle of public life, but it must be the constant resolute endeavor to give everything away that others may profit—there you have made manifest the inner Spirit, who only lives to pour himself out, and finds his satisfaction in the Service of man.

There, then, is the first great step. And wherever you see that, the person is approaching the Path, though he may never have heard of it. He is coming towards the Masters, though he knows not that They exist. There are some who are still in the twilight of unbelief in the spiritual life, who are nearer the entrance to the Path than many so-called religious men, who know the theory of religion but do not follow its practice. And there is one thing true of the value of the training of passing through a period of materialism—that in that there is absolutely no reward, no talking about the joys of heaven, nothing about "he that hath pity on the poor lendeth to the Lord, and lo, what he layeth out it shall be paid him again." In the life of the unbeliever, he sacrifices himself for man, and has no reward to look to, no return of outpoured riches to expect, and, in that, he gains a perfection of the sacrifice of the lower self that many an earnest Christian, Buddhist or

Hindu might envy him, in his depth and reality of life. There is an old friend of mine, twenty-one years passed away, whom some of the elder ones among you remember under the name of Charles Bradlaugh. There you have a man who had no belief in the life of the other side of death, who, dying, remained with the idea that death for him ended everything, that nothing was left save any work he might have done for men. And I know of no more spiritual statement—aggressive Atheist as he was—than a passage that he uttered when he spoke of the citadel of human liberty and happiness, that in the future he hoped humanity might reach, though he believed he would never see it for himself. "Enough for me," he said, "if my body, falling into the ditch that keeps humanity from its future, may act as a bridge over which others may tread to the happiness that I shall never see." The man who could say such words, with the depth of belief that distinguished all which was his, was a man who was taking the first steps to the Path, which, in another life, most surely he shall find.

Learn, then, that the service demanded is that unselfish service that gives everything and asks for nothing in return; and if you find that in you it is a necessity of your nature, not a choice but an overmastering impulse, then you may be sure that you are one of the men of the world who are taking the first steps towards the Path. (I need hardly say that when I say men I mean women too, but I cannot keep on saying "man and woman" each time, as it makes such difficulty with the pronouns)!

Take that, then, as the first and the most vital step. And there is another that may strike you as a little strange, and yet it is true. The man who can become possessed by an idea, so that no argument, no personal advantage, none of the reasons which influence ordinary men can turn him away from the following of that idea, that man is coming near to the Path. The great Indian psychologist Patanjali, who wrote certain axioms of Yoga, described in these the stages of the life of man through which the mind of man passed. And he said there was the butterfly stage, the stage of the child, in which the mind ran from one thing to another as the butterfly hovers over the flowers, taking a little honey here and there, ever changing the objects it turns to, seeking pleasure, amusement, delights, everywhere. That butterfly mind, he said, is far from Yoga. And then there was the mind of youth, as he considered it, the mind that is impulsive, under the sway of the emotions, rushing everywhere, possessed as it were for a moment with an idea but then possessed with another, more steady than the butterfly mind, but still varying in direction although holding strongly for the time. That, he said, is far from Yoga. There was then the stage when the mind became possessed by an idea, obsessed if you like, but so gripped and held that nothing could turn aside the man from its following. Now, if that idea be a true idea, turning to the Service of man, consonant with natural law, such an idea-possessed man is near to the entrance to the Path. I am not forgetting that the fixed idea may be the fixed idea of the maniac; but then it is a false idea, not a true one; then it disregards the laws of nature, is not in accord and in harmony with the law of evolution, which is the law of progress. But in studying the maniac with his fixed idea, you may gain some light on what it means when we say a man is possessed by an idea. You see it in enthusiasts, in heroes, in martyrs. When a man like Arnold von Winkelried rushed upon the pikes of the enemy and drew as many as he could into his arms and turned the points into his own bosom, in order that a gap might be made in the opposing force through which his comrades might pass when he lay dead on the ground, he was possessed with the idea of helping his country, and—when it was a question of his country's liberty—love of life, fear of pain, that influence ordinary men, had no power to change him. And so with the martyr, the man who dies rather than tell what he believes to be a lie. It does not so much matter whether he is right or wrong. Many men have been martyred for what they believed to be true, but which was error. That matters not so far as this possession is concerned. When a man so believes a thing to be true that it is easier for him to die than to deny his truth, the man deserves the name of martyr; and the crown of martyrdom is a knowledge afterwards of the truth. It is the attitude of the man that matters. I will take another point which will show you that I am not putting this merely as thinking of things with which I thoroughly agree myself.

One of the burning questions of the day is the policy which is being followed now by the extreme party in Women's Suffrage. On that policy it is no duty of mine to express an opinion; when I am not taking part in a thing, I never judge those who are facing a danger that I do not share. But I say it does not matter whether the people concerned honestly in that are right or wrong. It does not matter whether they succeed or fail. It does not matter whether their judgment is accurate or foolish. These questions do not touch the character, the life, that is being builded by the heroic sacrifice and the splendid devotion which are sending gentle, refined and cultured women into the hell of the police court and the prison.

I have taken that case because in any audience you will find much difference of opinion as to the wisdom or the folly of the *action,* and I want you to realize that from the occult standpoint the outer action is as the husk which is broken and cast away, and within the husk the fruit of the *motive* is seen: nobility of character, heroism and courage, perfection of self-devotion. And when you find people thus possessed by an idea, so that no worldly argument suffices to shake them, then I tell you, by that great occult rule which many of us know to be the truth, they are approaching the gateway of the Path. For the errors of the brain may be corrected rapidly, almost in a moment, but the building of heroism, devotion and self-sacrifice is the work of many lives of strenuous endeavor. And it is in that way that Occultism judges of all these things in the world. The outer action is the expression of some past thought, some past emotion; the motive for the action is what is all-important. And so, looking around over the world, we do not judge the place of men by action, but by thought, by will and by emotion. Those are the things that last, while actions rapidly pass away.

I do not know if, without seeming for a moment to be too personal, I might tell you one incident in my own life which, as Madame Blavatsky told me, brought me in this special life to the Portal of Initiation. As a matter of fact, it did, and it was a great blunder, a great mistake; and I mention it the more willingly because it was a mistake and not a thing that as an action was wisely thought or wisely done—the defence of the Knowlton Pamphlet, backing up a wretched little pamphlet whose author died before I was born, which no one could be proud of, no one could like, merely because I thought the suffering of the poor would last longer, unless the question of population was allowed to be discussed. I know that in these days thousands of people are on that side. Then they were not. It meant social disgrace, apparently social ruin, especially for a woman; and it was about as wrong-headed a thing as anybody could have done, looked at from the standpoint of the world; and that is why I mention it. Everything was wrong, except the desire to lessen the sufferings of the poor and the willingness to suffer for that object; but because that was the motive, because, for the sake of the poor, I flung aside everything that a woman values, therefore it brought me to the Gateway of Initiation in this life. You could not have a more extreme case.

You see then why I say that the occult rule judges of the motive, and not of the outer action in which that motive materializes itself in the world of men. And it did not matter one bit that one of my earliest actions after coming into the Theosophical Society was to repudiate utterly the whole of that theory—logical from the standpoint of materialism, but impossible from the standpoint of spirituality. That was my test.

Realize, then, friends, that what you have to study is your motive more than your action. Make your actions as wise as you can; use your best thought and your best endeavors to judge what is right before you do it; but know, for your comfort, that the eyes that scrutinize not the outer face but the heart, judge by a better judgment than the judgment of the world. Give yourself wholly to Service, keeping nothing back; help, wherever help is possible; work, wherever opportunity of work is seen; give yourself to some great ideal; follow it through cloud and sunshine; walk by it in storm and in peace. And when the lives that lie behind you have flowered in this life into such blossoms of service, of heroism, of devotion, then, man of the world as you may be, knowing nothing of the things of which we have been speaking, knowing nothing of the existence of the Masters and the glories of the occult world, you are beginning to tread those first steps which bring you up to the beginning of the pathway which inevitably will make you begin to seek the Master; but He will have found you long ere you begin to seek. Though seeking be necessary in the lower world, although the consent of brain and heart down here be necessary, and must be directed to the seeking of Him whose pupil one desires to become, know for your helping that the Master is there long ere you seek Him, that the Master is watching whilst still your eyes are holden; and while you think you are only serving man, while you think you are only helping the downtrodden, the miserable, the ignorant and the suffering, in the higher world where the judgment of the great Ones is made, Their sentence is pronounced, although you know it not: "Inasmuch as ye did it unto the least of these, my brethren, ye have done it unto me."

SEEKING THE MASTER

THE Sufis, who are the Mystics of Islam, have one exquisite saying that bears on that Seeking the Master which is our subject today. The Sufi Mystic says: "The ways to God are as many as the breaths of the children of men." That is true. Many are the different temperaments of men, many their different needs, and the cravings of men's hearts are as various as the satisfactions they desire. If we look at those many ways, those multifarious searchings for the true life, the life of the Spirit, for the Master Who embodies that life, we find that the many ways practically classify themselves into three great divisions, and along the one or the other of these we find the searchers, as they begin to realize the fact that they are really searching.

1 One is moved by an intense desire for knowledge, by the longing to understand, by the intellectual impossibility of happiness for him as long as the world remains an unintelligible puzzle, as long as the problems of life remain unanswered and apparently un-

answerable. Then another great class approaches the seeking by an intense love for some person who embodies an ideal, by loyalty and devotion to a leader in whom such a one sees embodied all that he most desires to realize in life. [A third great type has the will aroused in them by a realization of the intolerable anguish of the world, the terrible sufferings that press on so many of our race, the resolute determination to alter all that is alterable, and to refuse to believe that anything which man suffers is beyond the reach of man's remedy by the application of thought, of love, of activity. Those who are moved to the seeking by this realization of the sorrows of the world form the somewhat rebellious element in the great band of those who are engaged in the search for the highest.] And that way is perhaps the most familiar to myself, because it is along that way I sought and by that way I found. And that which oneself has experienced, the road that oneself has trodden, must always remain the most real, the plainest, the one which is easiest to explain to others.

In the past I have stood in the slums of this vast city at the moment when the closing hour had struck, and when the gin-palaces had belched out their flood of drunken, miserable humanity, the men raving, violent and cursing, the women sodden and miserable, clasping to their bosoms babes already poisoned with the curse of drink. I used to go down into the hells of the sweaters, where miserable men and yet more miserable women strive to win the right to starve alive—you cannot call it live. I have heard from the mouths of men a statement which is the sad explanation why economically women's wages are lower than the wages of men, when against the plea: "We cannot live on this," there has been reference made to that last sad resource of which none can deprive the woman—the selling of herself for bread. I have tramped through mud and slush at midnight to the meetings of omnibus drivers and tram drivers, the only hour they could find to consult with each other about some remedy for their poor wages. And out of all that there arose so keen a realization of human suffering, so passionate a desire to find a way in which that suffering might be cured, and finally such a despair of human effort, because these, the results of the misery, were scarcely fit to be builded into any better social state, that out of that there came the intensity of search for some way of redemption that might be found.

And so along one or the other of these ways a man may come, and truly has it been declared in an eastern Scripture: "By whatever road a man approaches me, on that road do I welcome him, for all roads are mine."

We find coming out in the poets, especially of the closing part of the nineteenth century, the different attitudes of those who seek in some way to remedy the sorrows of the world. You find the robust and cheery optimism of Robert Browning, who sings: "God's in His heaven; all's right with the world," forgetting, it seemed to some of us, that it is not the God in heaven that is so much needed, as to find the God in the hell of human misery. The words of the old Jewish psalmist strike there a better note of hope when he declares: "If I ascend up into heaven, Thou art there; if I make my bed in hell, behold Thou art there also." And that view that the responsibility is on God may tend to indolence, and then it is evil. But on the other hand one must not forget that there are thousands of the good and the earnest and the devoted, like the men and women in the Church Army and the Salvation Army, and in many another organization for the helping of the desperately poor, who find in that a source of encouragement and of inspiration. One cannot sometimes but wonder at the splendor of the faith that wells up against all reason, as it seems, from the unconquerable depths of the Spirit in the human heart, which is able to believe and work against all difficulty, and to believe in a God of love where the world bears such a multitudinous testimony on the other side.

And then we find another class who do not

take that view that I called a cheery and robust optimism, a gentler view, the view that Tennyson expresses in his famous *In Memoriam,* the view which hopes against all seeming and resigns itself to ignorance as the inevitable lot of man. You remember how he voices that which seems to be his own position, and which would scarcely perhaps stimulate to the Seeking the Master:

> Oh, yet we trust that somehow good
>   Will be the final goal of ill;
>   To pangs of nature, sins of will,
> Defects of doubt and taints of blood;
>
> That nothing walks with aimless feet,
>   That not one life shall be destroy'd
>   Or cast as rubbish to the void
> When God hath made the pile complete;
>
> That not a worm is cloven in vain,
>   That not a moth with vain desire
>   Is shrivell'd in a fruitless fire
> Or but subserves another's gain.
>
> Behold, we know not anything;
>   We can but trust that good shall fall
>   At last, far off, at last, to all,
> And every winter change to spring.

But it is not all who can remain contented with such a hope, who are content to say: "We cannot know;" and in those stormier natures, such as was my own, in face of the misery seen in those days to which I have alluded, the more passionate words of Myers seemed rather to express our attitude to life:

Were it not thus, O King of my salvation,
  Many would curse to Thee, and I for one,
Fling Thee Thy bliss and snatch at Thy damnation,
  Scorn and abhor the rising of Thy sun,

Ring with a reckless shivering of laughter,
  Mad with the woe which thou hast seen so long;
Question if any recompense hereafter
  Vails to atone the inexpiable wrong.

That is one of the ways in which man is awakened in order that he may really search; for there are natures whom very hopelessness of outside help throws back upon themselves to find what help may be, who say, in despair perchance and yet not all despairful: "There is no God, O Son, if thou be none;" who realize the beauty of the words of William Kingdom Clifford: "Is it said, 'Let us eat and drink for to-morrow we die'? Nay, rather, let us take hands and help, for to-day we are alive together." That will inspire a searching, that will stimulate to effort. The mental muscles are braced to struggle, to conquer in the end.

Those who by any of these ways have reached the point where they feel they must know, or perish, where they feel they must find a perfect ideal or lose all heart to live, where they feel they must find a remedy and not only an anodyne for human pain, they have reached the point where something shall come in their way to stimulate a conscious search for a Master, some perhaps apparently insignificant incident, which, none

the less, tells them how they are to seek.
Sometimes it is a book taken off a friend's
table while they are waiting for the coming
of a friend, a book, perchance, like Mr. Sin-
nett's *Occult World*, like any one of the Theosophical books that are lying about so widely
spread at the present day. And they, picking
it up and turning over the pages carelessly,
are caught, and begin to read, and then go on
to study, and begin to learn. Sometimes a
lecture, the man having strolled in carelessly
to get rid of an hour hanging idly on his
hands. Sometimes a picture, like the sugges-
tive pictures of the great artist Watts. Sometimes, where people are not likely to pick up
such a book, attend such a lecture, speak to
any friends on these great problems, it may
even come—as it came to myself—not by
book, nor picture, nor lecture, but by a Voice
that seemed to ring out within me and yet
without me, that was so clearly not my own
that, unthinking, I answered in spoken words,
as though speaking to one like myself. I was
in a City office late one evening, in that
strange silence of the City when all the human tide has ebbed away to the suburbs, and
you get that utter solitude which only this
crowded City knows in the quiet hours of the
evening. And in the Voice was something
that seemed to me, at the moment, a little
stern, clear, firm, exacting: "Are you willing
to surrender everything in order that you

may know the truth?" And all simply, un-questioningly, I answered: "Surely, that is all I need." But it went on, insistent: "Is there nothing that you hold back? will you let all go?" And again the answer: "There is nothing I will not surrender, if I can only know." And then the Voice changed into a music, full, as it were, of smiling and benevolent compassion: "Within a very little time the Light shall arise." And then again the silence fell, and I was left wondering what had occurred. But within one fortnight of that strange happening, Madame Blavatsky's *Secret Doctrine* was placed in my hands by Mr. Stead, then editor of the *Pall Mall Gazette*, with the request to review it, because it was out of the line of his young men's writing. I took the two great volumes home and sat down to read them, and read and read, hour after hour, until in very truth the Light had arisen, and I knew that for which I had searched through many weary years in vain. That is three and twenty years ago; and from that hour to this light has been thrown on the path of seeking and then of finding; for it is as true in the twentieth century as it was true in the first, and thousands of centuries before, that those "who seek shall find, and to him that knocketh it shall be opened."

So to many, in one or other of the ways, the knowledge comes, knowledge of the great facts I spoke of last week, of Reincarnation, of Karma, which explain the condition of things to-day, and which, applied to to-morrow, can remedy our social ills. For these give time and means of change; these offer not only the unriddling of the present, but help the creation of a nobler future; for you can apply them to the problems of education, of the most miserable and the most depraved, of criminology, of government, and understand the methods of change as well as the object to be aimed at. And to the seeker there comes first the theory, showing the truths on which the world is based, and by knowledge of the law giving also the means and possibility of change.

In addition to those two great fundamental truths, the other two I mentioned—the fact of the existence of the Path, and the fact of the existence of those who have trodden the Path, the Masters—answer to the heart and mind of the seeker, the longing not only to understand but to be an instrument of the working out of the Divine plan in human evolution. They tell the earnest seeker how he may tread the Path, how he may find the Master; and truly then does Light arise in the darkness, for you can see the steps before you for the taking, you realize the goal, although the goal be still out of grasp, even out of sight. When that word has gone out, as you find it in an old Hindu Scripture: "Awake, arise, seek the great Teachers, and

attend," then there comes from the mouth of the seeker the joyful answer: "I am awake; I have arisen; I seek the Teachers, and will not cease the search until I find." Then in the knowledge unrolled before him the whole theory of the seeking is laid down: how the man must search, what the man must do, the conditions that he must be willing to accept in the seeking, and the surety of the law that the seeker shall be recompensed by the finding. He discovers in his study that there is a science called the Science of Union, or the Science of Yoga, as it is phrased in the East, for Yoga only means joining, and the Science of the Joining leads to the great truth of the Union; and he sees then, stretching before him, the beginning of the Path, and learns the qualifications wanted for its treading.

What is this Yoga? It is neither more nor less than the application of the laws of evolution to the human mind and to the individual: the way in which the human mind evolves, clear and definite and under law; then how to apply those laws to the individual case, so as to quicken the evolution of the mind, and enable the man to outstrip his race, in order that thereby he may help it also to quicken its evolution. Yoga, then, means the application of these laws, and it joins to that a Discipline of Life.

Now, that Discipline of Life is necessary for those who would apply the laws of a swifter evolution to themselves, for the ordi-

nary laws of nature with which we are sur-
rounded carry us along ordinary evolution,
and if we increase the stress and the strain,
we must do something to strengthen all those
parts of ourselves which are subjected to the
strain in the swifter evolution that we are determined to follow. That is the reason for
the Discipline of Life. It is not arbitrary; it
is not, as some people think, an attempt on
the part of the Masters to build up obstacles
on the road that leads to Them, obstacles
which people will be unwilling or unable to
overclimb. It is a necessary guarding of the
would-be disciple against the dangers of his
swifter progress, because of the great strain
on body and on mind that that swifter progress entails. And unless you are able to
realize the common-sense of that, unless you
will admit, as every seeker for the Master
must admit, that he is demanding to do in
brief space of time what his race will take
hundreds of thousands of years in the accom-
plishing, and that therefore, if for no other
reason, he must prepare an at present unpre-
pared body, an untrained mind, for the huge
task to which he is addressing himself—unless he can realize that, it is better not to go
further than the point we have already
reached—the merest theoretical knowledge
of the fundamental truths, the facts of the
Path and of the Masters. When you turn
from theory to begin practice, when from

learning, as you might learn any science out of text-books, you turn, as it were, to the experiments of the laboratory and begin yourself to handle the chemicals, yourself to build up the compounds, yourself even to make new researches, then, as you know well enough, the student needs a guide, a teacher, a helper; otherwise, taking up for himself that which the majority leave aside, unknowing the conditions, he may injure, maim, kill himself, because he is affronting dangers that the great majority of the race leave on one side.

Now, the Science of Yoga has its own practices and experiments, and therefore its own dangers. If you believe it possible that there should be such a science, if by study you have convinced yourself that such a science exists, it is childish to kick against the restrictions which every science places on its students until they have learned and understand; and then they can go forward as they will, for knowledge has justified their independence.

This Discipline of Life does, I frankly admit, keep off a certain, even a considerable, number of those who say that they would like to enter on the search which means presently to tread the Path. People sometimes more resent restrictions on their ordinary daily life than they resent things more impalpable, and therefore less realized. Take, for instance, one very common habit, especially of the western world, and now unhappily penetrating into the East, the habit of taking various forms of alcoholic drink. I admit that for the great majority of men and women of the world, leading the ordinary life of men and not inclined to fall into the excesses which we see amongst the less cultured and less intellectual, very little harm accrues from the taking of a certain small amount of wine or spirit. I admit men can do it all their lives, and women too, with very little harm. Those of them who adopt abstinence without desiring to follow Yoga probably do it because they see the harm and the excess drink leads to, and realize that example is better than precept. Those who take it will injure themselves a little. But then they are injuring themselves all the time by insanitary habits, and one, more or less, is not a matter of life and death. It may shorten life a little; it may open a small door to let in disease. But it is quite different when you begin the practice which by seeking leads you to the Master; for part of that practice is what is called Meditation, concentrated, definite, hard thinking along a particular line, which is intended to stimulate and develop in you organs at present rudimentary, which will not develop in ordinary people in the ordinary course of evolution for a considerable time, although I admit a good many amongst ourselves are just beginning to evolve them. Now those organs are in the physical brain, organs which doctors have lately stated are peculiarly susceptible to any vapor of alcohol, which by it are poisoned, and so are rendered incapable of functioning healthily at all. When you begin deliberately to hasten their evolution from the rudimentary or semi-rudimentary conditions up to the activity in which they become the bridge between the physical and the astral worlds, by means of which you bring through certain vibrations to which the rest of the brain does not ordinarily respond, the organs, which are literally the bridges of communication; then, by thus increasing the flow of blood to them by meditation, thus stimulating the minute vessels which feed them, you will render the danger of inflammation very much greater; it is madness to do it, if those organs are already suffering from slight alcoholic poisoning, which, while it goes on without bringing much harm where the organs are left alone, becomes a source of active and serious danger the moment they are stimulated to growth, the moment attention is turned towards them in order that they may develop. Hence part of the Discipline of Life for the practical study of Yoga is the entire putting aside of every spirituous liquor.

Another demand which is made, still more annoying in the minds of many—and I grant it is troublesome to those who are very much in contact with their fellows—is the dropping of all forms of flesh food. That does not poison in the same way, but it tends slightly to coarsen the body, and the aim of the student of Yoga is to have a body which will be very strong and very resistant, while at the same time it is very sensitive and very responsive to vibrations from the subtler worlds of matter and of life. You have to deal here with your nervous system and your brain; you have to build those up; and the building depends upon the kind of food that you take; and, putting aside all questions of compassion (though they cannot be put aside by those who would seek the Masters of Compassion) and taking only the physical results, apart from any question as to animal suffering and pain, you find that unless your nerves, your brains, are prepared, that the vibrations of subtler matter beating upon them—and you are inviting that beating, remember—will tend to disorganize both, and to render you liable to nervous disorder and to various forms of hysteria.

This warning I am bound to give. If you want to see it justified, turn back to the records of Mystics and Saints, whose religions did not impose upon them a strict Discipline of Life. You will find much of unbalanced thought and judgment, much of hysterical emotion, mingled with a splendid insight into the worlds called invisible, and a marvellous response to the powers coming from beings of the higher world. That is so unchallenged, so unchallengeable, that some psychologists have used it as a proof that all religious higher vision is really a form of hysteria, and that all great Saints and Prophets and Teachers of religion are more or less unbalanced, when they have come into touch with the invisible worlds. You know how far Lombroso went in that, and many of his school go as far as he did. If you would search safely, if you would keep your balance, your nervous system strong and sane and healthy, then you must be willing to pay the price that all have paid in the past and are paying in the present, that when they affront those keener vibrations, when they allow them to play upon their body, and especially on the brain and nervous system, they must then take up a life different from that led by men and women of the world, and must be willing to tune up the instrument on which the melodies of the Spirit presently are to be played.

So you may take Yoga practically to cover an application of the laws of mind to swifter individual evolution, and a discipline of life —the latter applicable, of course, to those who practice, who do not only study.

Then the seeker finds that there are certain Qualifications laid down for the treading of the earlier portion of the Path, that which the Roman Catholic calls the Path of Purgation, which the Hindu and the Buddhist call the probationary or preparatory Path. Those Qualifications are laid down quite plainly and definitely, so that any man may begin to practice them, and the practice of them, with some slight restriction which I will give you in a moment, need not imply that Discipline of Life of which I have been speaking, because it does not, with one exception, lead into a certain definite practice of meditation. These Qualifications are said to be four. First the Power to Discriminate between the real and the unreal. I shall go more fully into these next week, but I want to run over them now to show you the line of the preparation. You have to learn to distinguish in everything around you, and in everyone around you, between the permanent element and the impermanent, between the surface and the content, as it were, between the eternal and the transitory. That is the first of the Qualifications, and that leads on necessarily to the second; for when you distinguish between the passing and the lasting, you become somewhat indifferent to the things that are everchanging, while your gaze is steadfastly fixed on that which you recognize as lasting. The second Qualification is what is called Dispassion, or Desirelessness, the absence of desire for the fleeting and the changing, the concentration of desire on the Eternal, on that which Is. The third Qualification is made of the Six Jewels, mental qualities that you must ac-

quire. First, Control of the Mind, that you
may be able to fix it steadily on a single thing,
to suck out all the contents of that thing, and
also to use it as an instrument in the building
of character; for your mind is your only instrument, remember, whereby you can create, re-create yourself. As the mallet and the
chisel in the hand of the sculptor, so is control of the mind moved by will the mallet and
chisel in the hand of the man who would create out of the rough marble of his own nature
the perfect image of the Divine that he seeks
within that marble. Then Control of Action,
which grows out of the mind, and the great
virtue of Tolerance. No one who is bigoted,
narrow-minded, illiberal, can enter on the
Path we seek. Tolerance, broad, all-pervad-
ing, that is one of the Qualifications, and it
means far more than some of you think. It
does not mean the spirit that says: "Oh, yes,
you are all wrong, but you can go your own
way." That is not real tolerance; that is
rather indifference to your neighbor's wel-
fare. The real tolerance grows out of the recognition of the Spirit in the heart of each, of
him who knows his own way and takes it,
"according to the Word," recognizing in each
the Spirit that knows, seeking in each the will
of the Spirit that chooses, never desiring in
any way to compel any more than to obstruct;
to offer anything we have of value, but never
to desire to force it on the unwilling; to place

what we believe to be true before the eyes of
another, but to feel no vexation, no anger, no
irritation, if to him it is not true; to remember that truth is no truth to anyone until he
sees it and embraces it for himself, and that
we are so built, our inner nature is so true,
that the moment we *see* a truth we embrace
it. It is not argument, but recognition, with
which the Spirit in man meets the unveiled
truth, and while the bandage is on the eyes
and we cannot see, truth is to us as falsehood,
for our nature has not recognized it as truth.
That is what tolerance means, holding your
own, willing to share it, but ever refusing to
impose or to attack. The fourth jewel is Endurance, that strong power which can bear
without giving way, which can face all things
in the search for truth, and never fall back
because of difficulty or peril; which knows no
discouragement, admits no despair, which is
sure that truth is findable, and resolute to
find it. Every obstacle makes it stronger,
every struggle strengthens its muscles, every
defeat makes it rise again to struggle for victory. The man needs endurance who would
tread the higher path. Then Faith, faith in
the God within you, faith in the God manifested in the Master, faith in the One Life
whereof we all are manifestations, faith unshaken and unshakeable, so that no doubt
may arise. Then Balance, equilibrium. The
Song Celestial says: "Equilibrium is called

Yoga;" absence of excitement, absence of passion, the transmutation of excitement and passion into the will that points unswerving to its goal; the power of standing serene while all around are troubled; the power of standing alone where all others have left and have deserted. That perfect balance is the sixth of these jewels of the mind. The fourth Qualification is the desire to be true, the will to be free, in order that you may help.

These need not be wholly gained before you find the Master, else were the search well-nigh impossible. All that is meant by saying that these are the Qualifications is that you must aim at them, and try to begin to build them into your character. You build so much better if you know what you want. You study so much more effectively, if the subjects of your examination are before you. And so these are laid down by the Masters as the Qualifications that those are to develop who desire to find Them and to become Their pupils. The moment we know them we can begin to work at them. The moment we see them we can begin to try to develop them, and only a little development in each is wanted before the search will pass into the finding.

But you may say: "How begin, how work at them?" Not by that vague wish to be better than you are, which is all that some people seem to know of the deathless, unconquerable will which forces its way to the Path. The means are very largely meditation, and then the practice in life. There are no other real means for meditation is concentrated thought, and concentrated thought is, as I have just said, your one instrument when you would re-create yourself. For this meditation to be safely practiced, it is necessary to adopt the Discipline above mentioned. Meditation means that you will for a time withdraw from the world, not for long at first, for it is a strain upon the brain; five or ten minutes in the morning is enough to begin with, and if you have done it well you will find it enough, for you will be tired before the ten minutes are over. For that time you withdraw from the outer world, you shut it right out, you build a wall, as it were, around you, through which the thoughts and the hopes and the fears of the outer world cannot pierce. You go within yourself, into the Holy of Holies within you, and there you sit, in the silence within that wall, to listen for the voice of the Self, to await the coming of the higher man into his kingdom. And when you have built your wall and shut out the outer world, you turn your mind, which is ever wandering about and disturbing you, and fix it on some single idea. Take, if you will, the first of the Qualifications, in many ways the most difficult—discrimination. You begin steadily to think of what that means, to think, say, of yourself; you realize that there is much in you that is changing and not permanent; your body is changing; your emotions are changing; your thoughts are changing. Those then belong to the unreal and not to the real, and in your thought you put those aside, sometimes one by one, sometimes with the body; you put aside a single sense like that of sight, and try to realize the world as it would be without the sense of sight, or any other sense that you please for the time, to force yourself into realizing that it is not yourself. You feel an emotion and put it aside, shut it out, refuse to vibrate in answer to it, and you see those changing emotions are not yourself. Then those wandering thoughts that change with every breath; you put them aside, and see that changing phantasmagoria of thought is not yourself. And so you shut out part after part, until perchance nothing seems left, for you find that all is changing, and you seek the real and the changeless. But in that emptiness that you have made, in that void whence the unreal has disappeared, from which the changing has vanished, and where for a moment you feel disappointed, in that void there arises upon you the higher consciousness, the deathless, the unchanging, the eternal; the Will, of which your changing wishes are the reflection in the lower world; the Wisdom, of which your varying thoughts are the images in the lower world; the Activity, of which your changing actions are the

reflection in the lower world. You feel yourself to be Will, Wisdom, Activity, apart from
all those changing images. Just as the sun in
the heaven is unchanged, but is mirrored as a
thousand suns in ponds, lakes, rivers and
oceans, so do you know the Sun of the Spirit
within you from the broken reflections that
you find in the lower self. You gain by meditation the knowledge that you are eternal,
and that all the changing things are only the
broken images of your real Self.

Out of that quiet meditation, out of that
great realization, you go into your outer
world of broken images, and you try to live
in the Eternal while you are busy in the outer
world. You know you are dealing only with
reflections, but reflections of vital import for
the building of character and for the helping
of men. You know there is something beyond them, and that in yourself, but willingly you go out into the world of men to bring
them what you have found in the silence of
the chamber of life. You live what in that
chamber you have known; you walk in the
light which there has risen upon you; you
love with the love that grows out of the love
of the real, and you become a true worker in
the haunts of men. And so, again, it is written: "Yoga is skill in action," for only the
man who knows the higher can control the
lower; only the man who is without desires
can see how to work best for the helping of

his brethren; only the man who has the will that never changes can be unmoved by the passing wishes that flit through the lower nature.

From meditation to work, from the gaining of light to the bearing of it into the world, from the learning of wisdom to the using it among men, from the realization of right activity to the guiding aright your acts. And as the man thus searches, desiring to find the Master, as he offers to Him the service he is able to render and works with the longing to find Him that so he may serve Him better, then after long seeking and resolute searching he sees awakening in his partial darkness the Light that is real; he comes to the point where the Master will find him, where truly his feet shall be set on that probationary Path, for which he has been preparing himself during his search.

And so we leave him knocking at the door, seeking for the Master, knowing that the door will soon be turned upon its hinges, and that on its threshold the Master shall be found.

FINDING THE MASTER

WE left our aspirant last week on the threshold, as it were, of the door that opens into the presence of the Master. He has served in the outer world; he has learned theoretically of the existence of the Path and of the Masters; he has acquired a certain amount of knowledge as to the great facts of human life and human evolution; he has awaked to the wish to take himself definitely in hand, to use the great laws of nature in order to quicken his evolution that he may be of greater service to the world. I ran over very hastily the names of those Qualifications which are definitely laid down as precedent to Initiation, not that they must be perfectly acquired, not that the man must show them out without failure in their full strength and full beauty, but that he must have made some progress in weaving them into his character, must to some extent at least have shaped his conduct after these main ideas of Right Living—right living as laid down by the Masters of the Wisdom as necessary for candidates for the Path. I told you also something of meditation, as the means whereby a man may create himself, first thinking of the ideal and then carrying it out in life. I must ask you just to recall those closing sentences of the last lecture, because, in the brief time I have to cover a big subject, there is not leisure enough to repeat.

And now I must go straight on to the Finding of the Master, and the living out of those Qualifications in action along the lines that the Masters demand. It may well be that on some of the points your thought may not wholly accord with the thought of the Occultist; it may be that on some points you may think too much stress is laid on something that to you is trivial, while on the other hand some things are omitted that you may regard as essential to right conduct. But we are now passing out of the region of opinions into the region of facts. The disciple cannot choose the Qualifications; it is his to fulfil them; and if he thinks them ill-chosen or unnecessary, there is no obligation upon him to enter on the Path of which they are the preparatory stage. Only, if he would enter on the Path, the Guardians of which are the Masters of the Wisdom, then he must accept the conditions that They lay down; he must endeavor to shape himself according to the immemorial law of the disciple.

When a man has sufficiently distinguished himself by service, and by acquiring and accepting the theoretical views that were glanced at in "Seeking the Master," then he finds his Master—or rather his Master finds him. During all the time of his struggle those gracious eyes have been upon him watching him progress; in many lives in the past he has come under the same influence which now is to become the dominant influence in his life. He has reached a point where the Master can reveal Himself, can place him definitely on probation, can help to prepare him for Initiation. That is the first stage: a particular Master chooses a particular aspirant and takes charge of him, in order to prepare him for Initiation; for you must remember that Initiation is a quite definite thing, that only Those who have already attained can enable others to enter on the Path which They Themselves have trodden.

Now, the time has come for the knitting firmly of the link which cannot be broken—the distinct individual tie between the man who is still outside the Path and the One who stands at its summit; a tie which shall endure from life to life; a tie which nothing can break, neither death nor failure nor folly; it holds against all attempts to break it. The man may go slowly towards his goal, but he can never entirely break away, nor can he utterly fail. The tie is there, knit and knotted

by the Master, and there is no power in all
this universe which can break that which a
Master has made. He summons the man to
His presence—not, naturally, in the physical
body, for, for the most part, the Masters live
away in retired places difficult to reach, hard
to find. But long before this the man has
learned, when the body is sleeping, to work
actively in the world invisible to fleshly eyes,
and in what is called his astral body; which is,
remember, the lowest of those invisible bodies
above the physical, in which the whole man is
present, Spirit and soul, clothed in a subtler
body; it is in that that he receives the summons of the Master to enter into the Master's
physical presence, to stand face to face with
Him and listen to His words. Then that Master places the man on what is called "probation." It means the knitting of the tie I have
spoken of, and then the sending of the man
back into the outer world to see how he will
live his life, how he will meet his trials, where
he will show strength and where show weakness, to test how far the strength admits of
the rapid working out of the evil karma that
may still exist. He comes back to the world
a disciple on probation, feeling a new strength
behind him, a new power encircling him;
knowing, even though he may not remember
the event, that some great thing has happened to him on the inner planes of being;
for the strength of the Master is with him;
the blessing of the Master is upon him; the

hand of the Master is stretched out in blessing over him; and so he goes to his probation
in the world of men.

Quickly or slowly, according as that probation is lived nobly or poorly, another summons comes to him, when the Master sees
that he has gained to a considerable extent
the Qualifications which are necessary, and
needs a further fuller teaching in order that
he may apply his knowledge more efficiently
to life. Again he is called; again he sees his
Master. And then the Master accepts him as
disciple, no longer on probation, but accepted
and approved; now his consciousness is to
begin to blend with the consciousness of his
Master, and he is to feel His presence more
clearly, His thought more effectively.

It is very often at that stage that special
and illuminating teachings are given to the
young disciple, in order to help him more
swiftly on his way. Such you may read, if
you like, in the little book that I hold in my
hand, called *At the Feet of the Master*, in
which a young disciple, taught by his Master,
on his return to the body wrote down, day
after day as best he could, that which his
Master had told him of the way of applying
the Qualifications to life, and of understanding thoroughly what those Qualifications
meant. So far as I know, it is the first time
that anyone has been allowed to write down,
word by word, teachings received on the in-

ner plane along the lines of the Qualifications. I do not mean that nothing has come from the great Teachers to the world, but this is peculiar, inasmuch as the Qualifications are taken one after the other and their exact application to life is shown. And he who wrote them down has said: "These are not my words; they are the words of the Master who taught me; without Him I could have done nothing; but with His help I have set my feet upon the Path. You also desire to enter the same Path; so the words that He spoke to me will help you also if you will obey them. It is not enough to say that they are true and beautiful; a man who wishes to succeed must do exactly what is said. To look at food and say that it is good will not satisfy a starving man; he must put forth his hand and eat. So to hear the Master's words is not enough; you must do what He says, attending to every word, taking every hint."

In dealing with these Qualifications I am basing what I say on this direct teaching of one of the Masters of Wisdom and Compassion. Naturally, I cannot give you all that is written here, for that would far outpace my time; but the outline is taken from this special teaching, which I may remind you may be found, although not in this detailed application, in the Hindu and Buddhist books that have traced for us the preparatory Path as well as the Path itself. The names are given there; the outline has long been in our hands. It is the special application which may help any of you who know the names, but sometimes ask how they are to be applied to life. And it is that which I now go on to try to give you, though naturally in words feebler and less beautiful than those of the great Teacher Himself. For how should lips that still have the stain of earth upon them speak adequately those great spiritual truths, as they have fallen from the pure lips of a Master of the Wisdom?

The first of the Qualifications, as I told you last week, is called Discrimination, discrimination between the real and the unreal. Among the Buddhists they call it "the opening of the doors of the mind," a very graphic and significant expression. Last week also I told you how you might meditate in order to find the higher consciousness which is yourself. How shall we apply what we have learned in meditation to practice? To meditate on a quality and then to live it, that is the way of definite progress.

Now the Master makes one great division of the whole human race, sweeping and clear. He says there are only two classes of men in the world—those who know and those who know not. The second class naturally embraces at present the vast majority of human kind, for, as another Teacher said, few there are who are treading that narrow Path.

Knowledge, as He defines it, is the knowledge of the Divine Will in evolution, and the attempt to co-operate with that Will so as to help effectively forward the day when that Will shall be done on earth as it is already done in the higher worlds of being. To know then that the world is being guided towards a higher and nobler evolution; to know that every child or man, young or old, laggard or rapid in his progress, is walking by that divine Plan, and may be helped or hindered in the walking; to recognize the Plan and try to live in it; to make one's own will part of the Will divine, the only true willing there is; that is the characteristic of those who know. Those who know not this are ignorant.

Turning to apply that knowledge to practice, we are told how discrimination should be worked out in life, not only between the real and the unreal, but between all those many things in which there is more or less of the real, in which the essential mark of the real may be seen. And, first of all, we have to recognize that the form is unreal, while the life is real. It does not matter to the Occultist, to take an illustration, to what form of religion a man may belong. He may be a Hindu or a Buddhist; he may be a Christian or a Hebrew; he may be a Zoroastrian or a Mussulman. That is all of form and unessential; the question is: How does he live his religion, and how far does the essence of it come out in his thought and in his life? And so in distinguishing between the real and unreal in religion, we put aside the whole of the forms, admitting to the full that they are valuable to those who need them—they are the signposts that guide a man along the way of life—but knowing that they all mark out a single road, the road of man to Perfection. Not against any of them may the Occultist speak; not contemptuously must he ever look even at any forms that he may himself have outgrown; but he must realize that while forms are many, the Wisdom is but one, and the Wisdom is the food of the soul, while the forms are for the training of the body.

He must learn also to discriminate between truth and falsehood, not as the world discriminates, but as the Occultist discriminates. The man who is training his thought to truth and to the avoidance of falsehood must never ascribe to another man a motive which is evil as being behind an outer action. He cannot see the man's motive; he has no right to judge what he cannot know; and over and over again, as the Master points out, he may ascribe a wrong motive which does not exist, and so may break the law of truth. A man may speak angrily to you, and you, to whom the angry word is said, may think that the aggressor desired to wound or to hurt you, and see an evil motive behind the evil word. But

the man, it is pointed out, may not be thinking of you at all; he may have some troubles
of his own, some trials of his own, some strain
upon him of which you know nothing which
makes his nerves irritable and his lip-speech
unkind. Do not, then, ascribe a motive where
you are ignorant of it, for you are breaking
there the occult law of truth, and are con-
demned as a false witness before the bar of
the great Teacher.

You must discriminate also not only between right and wrong, for to the Occultist
there is no choice between right and wrong;
he is bound to do the right at whatever cost and at whatever sacrifice. He
cannot, as some will do, hesitate between the course which is one with
the divine Will and the course that goes
against it; that he left far behind him in his
progress towards the Path. He must ever
remember, in dealing with questions of right
and wrong, that for the Occultist there is no
excuse if he swerves from the law of right; he
must follow it more strenuously, more rigidly,
more perfectly, than the men who are living in
the outer world. To do the right is woven
into his nature, and no question can arise in
the mind as to taking the lower way when the
higher is seen. I do not mean that he may
not make a mistake; I do not mean that his
judgment may not err; but I do mean that
where he sees the right inevitably he must

follow it, or else his eyes will become utterly blinded, and he will stumble and fall upon the Path. But not only must he distinguish between right and wrong, but between that which is more or less important in the right things he follows. Sometimes a question arises of relative importance, and he must remember ever, when such question arises, that to serve the divine Will and follow his Master's guidance is the one important thing in life. Everything else must give way to that; all else must be broken in order that that may be preserved; for that Will marks out the path of the most important duty, and as he follows it the very best he can give is rendered to human service.

And then, in this distinguishing between the essential and the non-essential, he has to cultivate a gentle yielding, a sweet courtesy, on all matters that are not essential. It is well to yield in little things that do not matter, in order that you may follow perfectly those things that do matter. I remember myself how difficult at first I found it to check the wilful nature that I brought over from many other lives of struggle and of storm. And for a year or two I made it a practice never to refuse a single thing I was asked to do, in which right and wrong did not arise. I made it an exaggerated practice, in order rapidly to correct the inborn fault. And so I wasted a good deal of time, as people would say, in doing unnecessary things that people wanted me to do, in going out for a walk, perhaps, when I would far rather have stayed at home and read a book, yielding in everything in the immaterial in order that in the material I might go forward unswervingly towards the goal. And that I would recommend to those amongst you who are naturally imperious, naturally self-willed, for in the swing of the pendulum from one side or the other you must go sometimes to excess in the practice of the contrary, in order that finally you may strike the middle path, that golden mean which the Greeks said was virtue. And if you have little time and much to do, then it is well even to go to excess in the building of a virtue, in the eradication of a fault.

Then also you must learn to discriminate between the duty to help and the desire to dominate. There are so many people who are always meddling with the thoughts and actions of other people, and desiring, as it were, to save their neighbors' souls instead of attending to their own. As a rule, while you may offer help, you should never try to control another, save in those cases where they are placed in your hands for guidance; then it may be your duty to exercise some control over conduct. Along those lines the Master taught that discrimination should be practiced in order that this first great Qualification might become second nature to the disciple.

And then the second came, Dispassion, Desirelessness. That is very easy in its coarser forms. When once the great desire has arisen for the treading of the Path, the things that are unreal lose their attraction, the things that are seen to be passing have small power to hold back the man bent on going rapidly forward towards Perfection.

As it is said in an old Hindu Scripture: "The desire for the objects of the senses falls away when once the Supreme is seen;" when once the eyes have rested on the wondrous perfection and beauty of a Master, when the radiance of His character has shone out into the dazzled eyes, but one longing is left—to reproduce His likeness, and to be in some small measure His image, His messenger, among men.

But there are subtler desires that may trip up the feet of the unwary traveller. There is the desire to see the results of one's work. We work with all our heart and all our powers; we build our life into some project for the helping, the uplifting, of men. Can you, without a pang, see your project crumble in the dust, and the walls that you had built for shelter break down as ruins at your feet? If not, you are working for results, and not purely for the love of humanity; for if one has built ill instead of well—though meaning well—the great Plan breaks the work into pieces, and it is good. But the material is not lost. Every force put into it, every aspiration it embodied, every effort made in order to build it, are garnered up as materials for the raising more wisely of a greater building, which shall be according to the Plan of the great Overseer of the universe. And so we learn to work, but not to demand payment in results for our labor, sure that what is good must last, and willing that what is evil shall be broken.

Sometimes the desire for psychic powers attacks the disciple. "Oh, I could be more useful if only I could see; I could help people so much more if only I could remember what I do when out of the body." Who is the best judge, the disciple or the Master? Who knows best what is wanted, the pupil or the Teacher? If He sees you can help better by possessing them, He will open up the way and tell you how to build them. But sometimes the work is better done without them, the work of the special kind that He wants his Disciple at that moment to fulfil. Leave to Him the time when those powers shall flower; they are the blossoms of the spiritual nature, and they will come to open maturity when the great Gard-ener sees the time is come for the blossoming.

Not only do we desire results; not only do we desire psychic powers; but still subtler desires assail us—the desire to be looked up to, to be recognized as shining, the desire to speak and show our knowledge wherever we can. Let that go, the Master bids us, for silence is the mark of the Occultist. Speak when you have something to say that is true, helpful, kind, but otherwise speech is a snare and a trap. Half the harm in the world is done by idle speech. Not without knowledge did the Christ say: "For every idle word a man shall speak, he shall give account thereof in the day of judgment." Not evil words, nor wicked words, but *idle* words, He warned the disciple against. And to know, to do, to dare, and to be silent, that is one of the marks of the Occultist. So these subtler desires must also be weeded out and thrown on the rubbish heap, till only one strong will shall remain, the will to serve and to serve along the lines laid down in the divine Plan. So is the desirelessness accomplished, which the Buddhist wisely calls the "preparation for action."

Then come the six jewels I ran over to you last week—Control of the Mind, keeping the mind away from all that is evil and using it for all that is good. And that control of the mind is needed on the Path, for we must so shape our mind that it shall not be in any way shaken or disturbed by anything that the outer world knows as trouble: loss of friends, loss of fortune, evil speaking, slander, anything that causes trouble in the world. These, the Master says, do not matter. How far are most from recognizing that great truth. These are the fruits of past thoughts and desires and actions, the karma of the past working out in the action of the present. There is nothing in these to disturb you, but rather to encourage; for it shows that you are wearing out the evil karma of the past, and until it is outworn you are of little use in the Master's work. You must so control the mind that you shall think no evil, that you shall keep bright and cheerful as well as calm. You have no right to be depressed; it spreads a fog around you, causing suffering to others; and it is your work to increase the happiness of the world, and not to add your own contribution to its misery. If you are depressed the Master cannot use you to send His life through you to the helping of His brethren. Depression is like a dam built across the stream, preventing the waters from right flowing. And you must not build obstacles in the way of the Master's life that flows through the disciple, and so hinder His blessing from cheering the hearts of men. Right Control of Thought and then of Action, doing as well as thinking the right, the kind, the loving.

Then you must build up that great virtue of Tolerance, which is so rare amongst us. You must study, the Master says, the religions of others in order that you may be able to help them as otherwise you cannot. And yet the judgment of the world on that is condem-

natory and not approving. How often have I
seen the criticism directed against myself:
"Oh, Mrs. Besant talks like a Hindu in India,
and like a Christian in England." Of course
Mrs. Besant does! How else should she talk?
Talk Hinduism to Christians? But that would
not help them. Talk Christianity to Hindus
and Buddhists? But that would veil the
great truths from their eyes. Our duty is to
learn in order to help, and you can only reach
the hearts of men by sympathy when you can
speak from their standpoint instead of standing obstinately on your own. That is the great
mark of one who is truly tolerant, that he can
see a thing from the standpoint of another,
a d speak from that standpoint in order to
help.

Then you must learn Endurance, because
of those trials that I have spoken of that will
come raining down upon you in order that
your past karma may work itself out in brief
space, that you may be ready to serve. Take
trouble as an honor, not as a penalty; as the
sign that the great Lords of Karma have
heard your cry for swifter progress, and are
giving you the bad karma of the past that you
may exhaust it, and so are answering your cry.
Then you may endure cheerfully, and not with
a face of unhappiness and discontent; as it
is said of old that a martyr smiled in the fire,
regarding it as a chariot of flame that took
him to his Lord.

Then you must learn One-pointedness, or Balance, as the Hindu and Buddhist call it. One-pointedness in the Master's work, such balance that nothing can turn you aside from it.. As the needle points to the Pole and returns if forcibly dragged away, so must your will point unswervingly to that goal of the divine Will for human perfection, that you are endeavoring to reach.

The last of the six jewels is Faith or Confidence, confidence in your Teacher and confidence in yourself. But, says the Master, perhaps the man will answer: "Trust in myself? I know myself too well to trust it." No, is His answer, you do not know your Self; you only know the outer husk that hides it, for in the Self is strength unconquerable, that never can be frustrated or destroyed. And so the six jewels of the mind are gradually cut into shape, to be cut more perfectly in later years, but at least enough that they may be recognized in the character.

And then, ah, then, remains the last of the great Qualifications, the hardest of all, the one most likely to arouse opposition in the mind of many. The Hindu and the Buddhist call it Desire for Liberation; the Master calls it Union with the Supreme; and because the Supreme is Love, He brings it down to Love lived out among men. And as He deals with that great virtue of love, love which is the fulfilling of the law, He brands three vices as crimes against love, that must be utterly thrown aside by the disciple. The first is gossip, the second cruelty, and the third superstition. These, he says, are the worst crimes against love. And then He goes on to explain how it is so. He takes up gossip first, and points out how, in thinking evil of another, you are committing a three-fold injury on man; first, on the neighborhood in which you live, which you fill with evil thoughts instead of good thoughts, and so, He says pathetically, you increase the sorrow of the world. Then the evil thought about the fault of another, for if that fault be in the man your evil thought makes it stronger, and harder for the man to overcome; your thought makes the evil in him greater every time that in thought you ascribe that fault to him, and you are thus making your brother's path more difficult, making his struggle harder; perhaps your evil thought will be the last determining push which makes him fall, where otherwise he might have stood upright. If the thought be false and not true, even then in him you may plant an evil which as yet does not exist in his character. Hence the wickedness of thinking evil, let alone of talking it, for where an evil story is passed on to another, there the same cycle of evil is trodden by the one who was spoken to, and so you become a fountain of evil, careless as the words have been.

Cruelty He brands as another great crime against love, and He gives certain forms of it, so that the disciple may realize what he must avoid. Religious cruelty shone out certainly in days gone by in the murders and the tortures of the Inquisition; but the same spirit shows itself now in all harsh religious controversy, and in bitter words directed against those who are trying to think rightly, but apart from the thought of their fellows. Is it not the fact that the partial but lamentable withdrawal of our much-reverenced friend, Mr. Campbell, from so much of his work is due to the suffering inflicted on him by his ministerial brethren in the early days of his struggle for the right to speak the truth he knew? For the spirit of religious cruelty is not dead, although it no longer speaks in fire or in manacle.

And then He brands as another form of cruelty, vivisection. On vivisection Occultism speaks with a single voice, no matter what may be said in the name of science, no matter what Commissions may sit thereon and express their views; for cruelty is to do needless hurt to living things. The very Report issued by those pledged in defence of it admits that much of the cruelty has been useless, fallacious in its results, even while they say that where cruelty is not inflicted experiments may go on.

After the Inquisition and religious bigotry, after vivisection, a third great class He speaks of are those teachers who are cruel to the children that fall into their hands. Teaching is one of the noblest professions into which a man can go, but it offers also opportunities of wrong into which too many fall; the use of corporal chastisement, where a big, strong man ill-uses a weak and helpless child, that is branded by a Master of Compassion as one of the forms of cruelty that bar the way.

And the fourth class He mentions, I fear will have a difficulty in finding acceptance here—sport, where living creatures are sacrificed. Granted it is customary, that social opinion does not condemn it, that a man may slay thousands of living birds and not be called a butcher but merely a good sportsman, none the less that cruelty of sport is regarded as an obstacle for those who would tread the Path. And the Master points out that thoughtless cruelty brings about its work in misery and suffering as much as deliberate cruelty, which is comparatively rare. He points out that the law of karma does not forget, although man may fail to remember, and inevitably every pain inflicted on a sentient creature brings the reaction of pain on the one who inflicted it.

And then He marks superstition as the last of the crimes against love that He taught his young disciple must be utterly avoided.

But there was one point in connection with cruelty that although I left it out for a moment I must go back to, as it bears so much on the lives of you who are wealthier than those who work for you. He pointed out as cruelty —this has most bearing on India— the not paying of wage where wage had been earned. Though you will very seldom find it here, where the pay-day has become practically obligatory in all big industrial undertakings, Indian teachers have always spoken of it. The Prophet Muhammad said: "Pay your laborer before the sweat on his body is dry." The suffering wrought by that thoughtlessness is bitter and far-reaching. But a very common fault in the West, which comes under the same condemnation, is the leaving of bills unpaid for things by which others have to earn a livelihood. The women who labor with their needle, the men who are employed for men's clothing—these are sometimes driven well-nigh to starvation, because people of high rank, in great social position, forget the suffering they are inflicting, and the trouble they cause by the long taking of credit. That is one of the faults of society that the would-be disciple must turn aside from. Sometimes it spells bankruptcy to the trader, as well as starvation to those he employs.

The last, I said, was superstition. The Master speaks of two forms specially, one which still prevails, though much more lim-

ited than before, in the shape of animal sacrifice offered in some of the Indian temples—
mostly among the very poor and uneducated
in the villages more than in the towns. But
there are a few temples still left, I am
ashamed to say, where educated and thoughtful people offer up the blood of animals to the
divine Forms they worship. And the Master
speaks of that, and you will all join Him in
the condemnation. But your missionaries
will never persuade the Indians who still use
animal sacrifice—a minority as they are—that
animal sacrifice is evil, as long as far more
animals are sacrificed to the human palate
than are ever sacrificed in the temples. That
also is marked as superstition by the Master,
the cruel superstition, He says, that man
needs flesh for food. And it is a superstition,
as those know who have resolutely faced it,
and have learned that health and not disease
is the result of following the law of love. If
you think of that sometimes as superstition,
it may help you to put it aside. And at least
remember that in sending out preachers of
your faith to India, they will never move the
Indian heart where the kid offered to Durga
is blamed, and the kid sacrificed to the sahab
and the memsahab in the bungalow is thought
to be harmless; for they are a logical people,
and they say: "If we may not offer to God,
why should we offer to man? If the animal's
life is precious in the sight of God, as you tell

us, why do you take it away to put it on your own tables, instead of on the altar of the God?"

And so this great Teacher has traced out for us the Qualifications demanded for passing through the first portal of Initiation, for that Birth of the Christ in the human Spirit, which is the passing of that doorway. I have run over, roughly and inadequately I know, the wonderful teaching which comes from Him to illuminate us, but none the less you can see it is an exacting demand, none the less you will see how you must shake yourself free from many prejudices, customs, thoughtless ways of life, if you would find the Master and be reckoned by Him among His disciples.

May you be able to overclimb the obstacles custom, tradition, thoughtlessness, and habit have built up; may even such poor words as mine win you to the realization that there is no joy in life like the joy of discipleship, no so-called sacrifice that can be made which is not as the dross cast into the fire where gold comes out instead; oh! that in the hearts of even a few of you—one here and there scattered through this vast audience—the feeble words may light the eternal flame, and the passing movement caused by speech may grow into resolute will and a determined endeavor. Oh, then for you, too, in the near future there awaits the Finding of the Master, for you also who seek shall find; if you knock with the hammer of these Qualifications, surely the door shall swing open before you, that you may find Him, as I have been blessed enough to find Him, that you may know that service which is perfect freedom, that joy which is in the presence of the Master. That is the hope with which I would leave you to-day, that the aspiration that I fain would syllable for you. And let not, I pray, any imperfection in the speaker, any weakness in the disciple, dim in any way your view of that which shines with undying lustre, perfect with superhuman beauty—the figure of the Master Whom you may find if you will, so that you, too, shall say: "Having sought, I found."

THE CHRIST LIFE

WE have seen our man of the world taking his first steps deliberately towards the higher life; we have followed him as he sought for a Teacher; we have seen him succeed in the search, when the Teacher was found. To-day we have to follow him through the first of the great Initiations, onward along the Path until he reaches the entrance to the fifth. It is that life spoken of by S. Paul, of which the beginning is marked by the Birth of the Christ within the man. You remember how he wished for his converts that they should have the sublime experience that the Christ should be born in them. And then you may remember how he spoke of another stage: "Until," he said, "we all come unto a perfect man, the measure of the stature of the fulness of Christ." Thus did the great apostle of the Christian Church measure out the two limits of the study that we are to follow this morning—one the Birth of the Christ, the other the attainment of His full stature, the reaching of the Perfection of Manhood.

Such was S. Paul's idea of the meaning, the greatness, of the Path shown by Christianity. In modern days, I know, Christian ambition has not risen so high, and to be saved by another, to be clothed in the imputed righteousness of another, has been regarded as the Christian life. But the great Apostle saw otherwise what he called "your calling and election." Not to be saved by another, but to become a Saviour; that was the old and great ideal in the Christian Church; to be oneself a Christ; to lead the Christ-life; to pass through the great stages of experience marked out in the Gospel story, which, rightly read, is less the history of a Person, than a mighty drama of the Initiation of the Spirit. Looked at in that light, this high Path lies open, as that which should be trodden by all who would fulfil in their own persons the great hope of the Apostle for his spiritual children. That, and nothing less than that, is the possibility of all who will. It is this part of human life which is sometimes called quite simply "the Path;" sometimes, as among the Buddhists, "the Path of Holiness;" sometimes, as among the Roman Catholics, "the Path of Illumination," the Path on which the light of the Spirit is shining more and more unto the perfect day, that life which was led by the Christ as "the First-born *among many brethren*," and not as a unique proof of that to which divine humanity might attain. I grant to the full that this path is one which demands from the one who would tread it a total renunciation of all that in past lives he has held to be valuable and desirable. Hence it has been truly said: "Strait is the Gate and narrow is the Way, and few there be that find it." In ages to come many shall tread it; in ages far off all human beings shall know it; but humanity has scarce passed the middle point of its evolution, and hence few are they who at present are willing to tread the Path.

I used the word Initiation. I must pause on that for a moment, that it may convey to you some clear meaning; and I will ask you to recall what you all know from your own studies in the history of the past; that in all ancient nations there were certain great institutions known as Mysteries, with many other names to describe them, but all with that one word in common. Eleusinian, Orphic, Bacchic, whatever they might be, they were Mysteries, into which certain people were initiated. We are told that in the early days all those who were purest and noblest participated in these Mysteries; that they destroyed all fear of death, and gave to man the certainty of Immortality; that those who entered into them gained wisdom which others did not possess, and were marked out not only by the development of their intelligences, but even more by the nobility and the purity of their lives. They are recognized not only as existing in Greece, in Egypt, but also in Persia, in India, in China. And the two greatest of the Indian Teachers of religion were known as special expounders of the Mysteries, of the Path which led through them to the goal to which that Path conducted those who trod it. We have the great Teacher, the Lord Buddha on the one side, and the Buddhists still retain the details of the Path that He expounded. We have Shri Shankaracharya, the great Hindu Teacher on the other, Who also expounded the Path and marked out its stages in identical fashion. Then, turning aside for the moment from those great pre-Christian faiths, we find that in the early days of the Christian Church these Mysteries also existed. You may read about them in the writings of Origen and of S. Clement of Alexandria. You may learn from S. Clement how he cannot speak publicly of that which he learned in the Mysteries, but some of his readers will understand his allusions. You may read of that famous declaration which used to be heard in the Christian Church, when those who were worthy were summoned for admission to the Mysteries: "He who has for a long time been conscious of no transgression, let him draw near and learn the teachings which Jesus delivered in secret to His own disciples." And you may learn from other patristic writings how, in those Mysteries, Angels were sometimes the Teachers, and how they revealed the invisible world to those who were held worthy to become Initiates therein.

Although it be true that in our modern world the re-proclamation of the continued existence of Masters, of Initiates, of the Mysteries that have never disappeared, has been made specifically by the Theosophical Society (that being part of the work for which it was sent into the world), it does not pretend that in that re-proclamation it is bringing anything that is new to any great faith, but is only recalling to each great religion its own earlier knowledge and possibilities. If we say that the Mysteries still exist; if we declare that the Gateway of Initiation is still open; if we proclaim in the old world that those who seek shall find, that to those who knock the door shall be opened, it is not as making a new proclamation, but only as repeating a forgotten message—giving to a world that had been sunk in materialism the knowledge it had forgotten, on which it had turned its back.

Hence, to remind you that this is no specifically eastern teaching, but a universal teaching, I have spoken of the life of the Initiate in its Christian form, as the Christ-life. That is the name by which it was known long before the great Founder of Christianity came out into the world, for it is the life of the Anointed, of those who have been consecrated by the chrism of the Spirit, and have begun to tread the Path that makes them Priests and Kings unto God.

That is the ancient pathway called from very long ago the Way of the Cross; for the Cross is the symbol of life, of life triumphant over death, of Spirit triumphant over matter. And there is no difference in this Path between East and West; there is only one occult teaching and one Great White Lodge, the Guardians of the spiritual treasures of our race. They know no difference between East and West; They know no difference between white and colored; they recognize only Qualifications fitting for Initiation; and They open the Gateway in the old, the ancient, fashion, which allows a man to tread the narrow ancient Path.

Now what does this Initiation in the Mysteries mean? Quite frankly, it means an expansion of consciousness. Initiation itself is a certain series of events through which the man passes; actual events and experiences taking a certain amount of time, not a vague indefinite series of feelings, but actual communications and thoughts and actions gone through by a man out of the physical body, in the presence of a great assembly of the Masters. The result is that the man becomes conscious of a new world, as though some great new sense had been given to him which opened to him a new world surrounding him.

As a man born blind might know the world by hearing, taste, touch, but if his eyes were opened would see a new world he had not dreamed of stretching around him on every side, so is it with the man who, having passed through the great ceremony of Initiation, comes back into his body, into the mortal world of men. Another world is around him, a new phase of consciousness belongs to him. He sees, where before he was blind. He knows, where before he only hoped or guessed.

Of those great ceremonials on this Path there are five. The fifth is that of the Master, with which I do not deal to-day. Four are the Portals on the Path leading to that final divine Perfection of Manhood. It is to the study of those, then, that we turn. We can take four great events in the Christ-story related in the Gospels which, in the Christian symbolism, exactly represent that which has other names, but not other realities, in the Hindu and Buddhist descriptions of the Path. The first, as I have said, is the Birth of the Christ; the second, the Baptism; the third, the Transfiguration; the fourth, the Passion. Let us take them one by one, showing what lies under the names, and seeing how they are expressed among our eastern brethren. He in whom the Christ is born, the new Initiate, is ever spoken of, all the world over, as the "little child." You remember the phrases you meet with in the Gospel: "Unless ye become as little children, ye shall in no wise enter into the kingdom of heaven." The kingdom of heaven, or the kingdom of God, is the old name for the Path, and only the "little child" is able to enter there. The new Initiate, the Christ-child, then, is born into this new life of the Spirit, and the expansion of consciousness he attains consists in his having opened to him, for the first time, that great spiritual world in which all truths are known by Intuition, not by reasoning; in which the eyes of the Spirit are opened, and direct knowledge of spiritual truths is gained; knowledge becomes intuitive, instead of rational.

When the great ceremonial is over, then it is that, either by his own Teacher or by some high disciple to whom the work is delegated, the new Initiate finds open within him that new consciousness which is gradually to grow, so that he may master the knowledge which at first is only presented to him in a dazzling panorama. Because of that new world into which he is born, the first of the great Initiations is spoken of as "the second birth," the "birth of the Spirit." He has become now the twice-born—born on earth indeed many times, but always born into the life of matter; born now into the life of the Spirit, which becomes his for evermore. That is the key of knowledge which is said figuratively to be given to the new Initiate; it is a new faculty, a new power, a new sense, which has been gradually developing within him through the time of his training, and now bursts open into usefulness and comes under his control.

Then it is that that inner renunciation is made which you find typified in the three great vows that in the Roman Catholic Church, and in parts of the Anglican, are the vows which give admission to that which they call "the supernatural life." You know the vows of poverty, of chastity, of obedience. They symbolize a great spiritual truth: the inner renunciation by the new Initiate of the whole of the possessions, physical, mental, which hitherto he may have regarded as his own. Not by spoken words, but by inner renunciation, he gives up all sense of property, all sense of ownership in anything which he is supposed to possess. He may have wealth; it is no longer his—it belongs to the Great Lodge into which he is entering. He may have mental ability; it is no longer his— he must use it only for the service of that to which he has now given himself. And so from his heart departs all sense of ownership, all sense of property. And by a strange paradox, it is in that moment of utter renunciation that the Kings of the earth, the Wise Men, bring their treasures and pour them out at the feet of the helpless Babe; for where a man wants nothing, everything falls into his hands; and hands that are emptied in the service of the world are ever continually filled, although they never retain. So he not only renounces all possessions, and becomes thereby a steward able to administer in the work that lies before him, but he also renounces all pleasures of sense, the inner meaning of the vow of chastity. He surrenders also his own will, the personal will, the separate will, gives himself wholly to the one Will that is divine, and knows nothing save that Will hereafter, as the determinator of all he thinks, and hopes, and does. Such is the inner meaning of the great triple vow; renunciation of ownership, of all the pleasures of sense, of separate will.

And so he comes out again into the world. The Wanderer, the Hindu calls him, for he has nothing left to own. He wanders about, in the words of the Lord Buddha, "free as air," only vowed to the one service, and able to go anywhere where he is needed for the work. And the Buddhist calls him: "He who has entered the stream." He has stepped into the great stream of which the further side is Masterhood. He can never again step out of it, never again leave it; that stream rolls between the other world and this, and he who has once entered upon it must go to the other shore.

And three weaknesses he must get rid of now before the second Portal may be ap-

proached, get rid of them entirely, completely, utterly, for he can never again tread this
Path. Ever onward lies his way. They are
called three fetters, because they hold him
back until they are broken. First, the sense
of Separateness. He must see all around him
as part of himself, feel with their joys and
with their sorrows, look at things from their
standpoint, understand their feelings and be
able to sympathize with them—judge none,
criticize none. They are all himself, part of
his own life. The sense of separateness must
utterly pass away, for a Saviour of the world
must feel identity of nature with all. Hence,
no feeling against any as lower than himself,
no judgment of any as despicable or con-
temptible. He sees all as fragments of the
One Life, and identifies himself with each
in order to help and save.

He must get rid of all sense of Doubt—not
that rightful attitude of the mind to be doubtful of that which is doubtful, because at present unproved; that remains ever necessary,
else were there danger of credulity and folly
—but doubt as to certain great facts in nature.
The fact of Reincarnation he cannot doubt—
for now he knows his past; the fact of Karma,
the great law of action and reaction, he cannot doubt—he can look back and see its working in the past and trace it in the present; the
fact of the Existence of the Masters he cannot doubt—he has stood in that wondrous cir-

cle when he was initiated; the fact of the Path
he cannot doubt—he is treading it. Those
make up the doubt that for ever is left behind, the fetter which might prevent his progress.

The third great fetter is Superstition; the
belief that a particular rite or ceremony is
necessary for the attainment of the result that
by it is sought. He no longer needs the bridge
which a ceremony is intended to be to those
who cannot yet reach the higher worlds by
their own power, by their own knowledge. He
realizes that the ceremonies of all the religions
are equally useful for the adherents of each,
but that none are necessary for him. He knows
he can no longer depend upon any ceremony;
he depends only on the God within. Useful,
beautiful, helpful, as they may be to those
who have not passed the Portal, their value is
over for him, for he sees unveiled the realities
of the worlds which they can only symbolize,
and to which they bridge the way.

When those three fetters are utterly cast
aside, when they no longer have power to
hold him back, then he has grown to young
manhood, when he is ready to pass the second
of the great Initiations. In the Christian
drama it is called the Baptism. It is written
that the Spirit of God came down upon Jesus,
and abode with Him. That is the Christian
form; the Spirit comes down, the Spirit of
Intuition, and before he can go further, to the

third Initiation, he must learn to bring it down, through his enlarged causal and mental bodies, to his physical consciousness so that it may "abide on him," and guide him.[1] Hence the Hindu calls him the Builder, the builder of vehicles that he requires; the Buddhist: "He who shall receive birth once more," looking onwards to the goal towards which the aspirant is pressing.

After this Initiation the man has not to get rid of weaknesses but to add powers, all those superphysical powers which belong to the perfection of the superphysical bodies the man has now to create in himself, in order that he may more perfectly serve; for that great spiritual world, the intuitional world, is being conquered step by step, and he must be ready to serve in that, as in the mental and the emotional worlds. During the time that he stays in this stage of his progress, he is perfecting all the bodies, building them for the great work in front.

Short, as a rule, is that stage. And then he approaches the third great Portal, that which in the Christian story is called that of the Transfiguration, among the Hindus the Swan, the bird of heaven, the symbol of the recog-

[1] This process is usually called "the development of psychic faculties," and it is so, in the true meaning of the word "psychic." But it does not mean the development of clairvoyance and clairaudience, which depends on a different process.

nition of the "I" as one with God. In that the manifest Deity shines out, illuminating for a moment the Path in front, which is to go down into the depths of suffering, which is to lead him through the valley of the shadow of death; for you may remember that in the Gospel drama the Transfiguration on the Mount of Olivet is immediately followed by the steadfast turning of the face to Jerusalem, to the Garden of Gethsemane, the Mount of Calvary, the divine light shining on the darkness, that the human heart may be able to pass on, undaunted.

During the time which intervenes between the third and the fourth Initiations, two more weaknesses have to be got rid of for ever. Attraction and repulsion to all outer things. Attraction; you may see in the gospel allegory how the attraction was thrown aside of all that would hold the Christ back from the approaching Passion. And you may see how all repulsion had ended, when "the woman who was a sinner" was allowed to approach Him to bathe His feet with her tears, to wipe them with her hair; for attraction and repulsion for all external things must die before the last great trial comes, else would the road remain untrodden, else would the last ordeal be too great. And so the disciple learns in this stage to rise above attractions and repulsions, to cast them aside for ever; they no longer have power to touch him.

He prepares himself for the going to Jerusalem, for the betrayal by one Apostle, the desertion by all, the loneliness in which the last great sufferings have to be faced; for between the third Initiation and the fourth there is that gulf of silence, where the disciple hangs alone in the void with nothing on earth to trust to, nothing in heaven to look to, no friend whose heart can be relied upon—nay, even the vision of the Supreme blurred and dimmed. It is symbolized by the Agony in the Garden, where the human heart cries out: "If it be possible, let this cup pass away," and still the human will arises, strong in renunciation: "Nevertheless, not my will but Thine be done."

Onward he passes through the stages of the Passion; sees his beloved flee; sees himself betrayed, denied, rejected, until at last, upon the cross of agony, he is held up for all men to mock at, for all men to despise; sees at last no friend, but only a ring of enemies triumphant; hears the taunt: "He saved others; himself he cannot save"—the deepest truth of all; utters at last the cry of the breaking heart: "My God, my God, why hast *thou* forsaken me?" and in that uttermost loneliness finds himself for evermore; losing the God without him, he finds the God within. For when the great darkness comes down, and nothing can be seen, then arises the light of the Spirit in the human heart, and then through the darkness are heard the final words of triumphant success: "It is finished." Those are the words that ring out from the assembled hosts of Men made perfect and of Angels, when the great trial is over, and the agony of the cross is past.

Then the fourth great Initiation, that of the Arhat, the Paramahamsa—"He who is beyond the I am He,"[1]—is accomplished; he it is who has become the Christ crucified, and therefore the helper of the world; he has trodden the wine-press alone, and found in himself the strength divine to do it; he then awakens to the exquisite truth that loneliness for him is over for ever, for he has found the One Life and knows it evermore. He has conquered; and the rest of the path is comparatively smooth and easy.

After that fourth Initiation, the Passion, there remains only the Resurrection, the Ascension, which is the Initiation of the Master. And in the hidden life which intervenes between the Crucifixion and the Resurrection, the last weaknesses of humanity have to be cast aside. No longer can he desire life in any world, for he *is* life, and all outer desire passes away; from him also disappears that sense of being in any way "I;" he is all, and all forms

---

[1] There is no longer even the distinction between "I" and "He," but only the One. Beyond union there is unity.

are equally his own. No longer can he be shaken, for what can shake the life that knows itself? All may go, but all had gone before, and he had not perished. He knows there is nothing that can touch him, nothing that can shake him; he has become invulnerable to every weapon that might wound. He has become as the diamond, which nought may cut nor break.

And so from his eyes fall away the last remnants of the veil of ignorance. From him pass the last remnants of weakness, and he lives for the rest of that life in which he has become the Arhat, free as the birds in the air, his path trackless, his motives not understood; but what matters that to him on whom the light eternal is ever brightly shining? He lives as part of a mighty Order, part of a mighty force; he knows his work, and does it, and knows that the end is sure.

And so he works in this world and in other worlds—for now all worlds are open to him—having died to earth he has passed into Eternity, and the light is ever upon him, and the way is open. He only labors that others may share what he has gained, having won that most splendid of all rights, the right to help, whether the help be seen or recognized, or not. What is that to him? He has risen to that point where all men are open to him, and he can pour down strength, help, knowledge into all of them from that higher standpoint that now he has reached. And that it is to have become a Christ: to know the identity of nature which makes yours the weakness of the weakest, as well as the strength of the strongest; which makes yours the sin of the guiltiest, as well as the purity of the highest; which makes you share the foulness of the criminal, as well as the spotlessness of the saint. That is the true glory of Christhood, that the lowest is as loved as the highest, as much part of himself as the loftiest and the purest. For only those know the One Life, who can feel themselves in the worst as well as in the best, to whom all are as himself, all that he possesses theirs to take.

THE CHRIST TRIUMPHANT

THE long steep Path is trodden, and He who has climbed it, who has passed and assimilated all human experiences, He who has nothing more to learn in this world-system, who has faced the agony of isolation, who has passed for the last time through the gateway of death, He stands triumphant, with the door of the fifth great Initiation open before Him, great vistas of glory stretching beyond it. Nirvana, as it is called in the East, that all-embracing consciousness, that extinction of the lower self, and the full expansion of the Spirit, that stretches before Him, all-embracing, all-powerful, and there break from His lips the triumphant words: "Lo, I am He who liveth and was dead, and behold I am alive for evermore." Master of life and death, freed from every fetter that can bind, all power given to Him in heaven and in earth, He stands the Perfect Man, the cycle of humanity accomplished, the ideal of Divine Manhood fulfilled; in the language of the East, He who is liberated; in that of the West, He who has attained final salvation. The one of whom it was said that the Christ was born in him has now attained to the stature of the fulness of Christ. He stands among the many Brethren of whom the Christ is the Firstborn. He has "become a pillar in the temple of my God who shall go out no more." You catch in Christian and in Hebrew Scriptures from time to time a glimpse of such mighty Figures, as you read in the Hebrew Old Testament of that mighty One who was met by the patriarch Abraham, of whom it was written: "Without father, without mother, having neither beginning of days nor end of life, made like unto the Son of God, He abideth a priest continually." Such is the mighty triumph of the man who now has reached the Perfection of Humanity; the long past lies behind him, with its struggles, its failures, its successes. He has been born for the last time; over Him death has no longer power; He has become one of the Masters of the Wisdom; He has gained eternal life.

And now there stretch before Him, having accomplished His pilgrimage, seven paths that lead him onwards in the great realms of super-human life, seven paths of glory and of power, of which all, save one, free Him for ever from the burden of human flesh. Into mightier realms, where matter is but the obedient servant of the Spirit, thither may

He pass to work in the vast universe in which He stands now as King and Priest, and as He stands gazing at those seven pathways, He sees but one that turns back to the earth that lies behind Him, where the burden of the flesh must still be borne, where the weight of physical matter must still encumber, one path that keeps Him still to labor in the world, while the other six stretch onward, far away from our earth.

As He stands there, across the exquisite music which surrounds Him there sounds a sob of pain, a wailing from the earth that lies behind. He hears the cry of humanity in bondage; He sees the gropings of the ignorant, the helpless, and the blind. He sees the suffering that He has transcended, the weakness that in Him has turned to strength, the helplessness that in Him has been crowned into power. His race has cast around Him the only fetters that still have power to bind the enfranchised, the liberated Spirit; they are the fetters of compassion; they are the bonds of love; the old sympathy for the humanity of which He is the flower; for those who still lie in darkness and the shadow of death while Light Eternal is radiant around Him. And then He turns backward to the world that He had left. Then, instead of casting away the burden of the flesh, He takes it up and bears it still, in order that He may help mankind. The body which was the body of humiliation, and has become the glorified and spiritual body, He still is willing to wear, that He may not lose close contact with the humanity that He loves. And so, holding the mighty consciousness that He has won, but bearing still the burden of the flesh, He remains in the world that He has the right to leave, in touch with the humanity that cries out to Him for help. And so He becomes what we call a Master, a liberated Spirit who still bears the burden of the flesh. He it is, and such as He, rising in grade beyond grade of superhuman wisdom and power—He and such as He form the Occult Hierarchy, which consists of the Guardians of the world. They it is Who, remaining with us, remain to help, to guide, to strengthen, to uphold, so that humanity may not be without its Guides along the Path, may not be left to wander unhelped, unaided, in the difficult ways of human evolution.

He has become a Saviour of the world; He has gained the right and the power to help; for just as the sun pours down upon the world his light and life, as all life on earth is stimulated by his rays, as his warmth causes the seed to germinate, enables the plant to build up its substance, gives vigor and strength to the animal, and makes possible the life of man, so do these Suns of the spiritual firmament pour down upon earth Their strength, Their wisdom, cause to germinate all seeds of good in human kind, pour down life and strength that enable us to grow. They do not take our place; They cannot substitute Themselves for us; but by identity of nature, by the height at which They stand above us, They can pour down Their life to stimulate our growth, and our weakness becomes strength by the stimulus of Their power.

So They help the world, help it in ways that roughly now I will seek to outline for you. Three general ways there are in which the great life of the Hierarchy pours down upon mankind. From the great spiritual sphere Their light pours down in general benediction, like the light of the sun to which I likened it, illuminating and blessing all. All of you may profit by that, just in proportion as you are receptive to it, just in proportion as you are able to open your hearts to it, to breathe it in like the atmosphere that surrounds you. For as the sun shines, and you may open your windows and let the sunshine flood your rooms, or you may bar it out with closed shutters so that it may not illuminate and bring life and health, so is it with this widespread blessing of the Masters' life, which makes the spiritual atmosphere, which pours out as spiritual light. Open your windows and Their light shines in; it is beating against the shutters; and you have only to throw them open, and your Spirit will be flooded with Their light and strength.

And then there are great organizations, great communities, religious communities, into which a special Master will pour down His blessing and His strength. Made as vessels to receive the water of life, as mighty reservoirs to be filled in order that the water may be distributed, such are the great religions of the world; such these great spiritual vessels of many shapes, of many forms, but all containing the one spiritual water, for the quenching of the spiritual thirst of man. Into those organizations, drawn together for spiritual purposes, joined with the aim of spreading spiritual knowledge, a Master pours His life and inspiration, in order that they may distribute it to their adherents, so that they may give it to those within their pale. Hence the different religions of the world, with their different sacraments, or means of grace, adapted to the needs of the time for which they are given, to the temperament of the people on whom they are bestowed to shape and mould special civilizations, and so to guide and help the races and sub-races of men.

And in yet a third great way They help the thought of the world, sending out mighty thoughts of knowledge, of beauty, of inspiration. especially for those men and women of genius who have climbed to the point where they can be individually affected, and made, as it were, channels to the world at large; great thoughts of knowledge sent to the scientific genius; thoughts of beauty sent to the artist of genius; thoughts of patriotism and helpfulness to the statesman of genius; thoughts of mighty power to the literary genius, whether expressing himself in prose or poesy. These are the blessings sent out by the Masters of Wisdom for the helping and the raising of men; and never a great inspiration flashes into mind or heart, never some mighty thought illuminates a whole field of knowledge, never some exquisite form of beauty, whether for sound or vision, comes winging its glorious way into our earthly atmosphere but comes from that great Hierarchy that lives for the helping of man, ever plans new ways, works out new schemes, by which evolution may be quickened, by which the race may climb. Some of these take as pupils and disciples—along the lines by which I have already led you—take as pupils and disciples those who are willing to tread the Path that They have trodden, so that the ranks of the great Hierarchy may never be depleted, so long as men need helping, so long as humanity is dwelling on our globe.

From that more general and individual helping let us turn to two great departments of human life, in which the work of the Hierarchy is most especially to be seen, and in which all who have eyes to see may trace it as they will. There are two great departments of human life in which especially help is needed — the Ruling Department, which guides all natural evolution, changes the face of the surface of our globe, builds and destroys continents, raises fresh races which grow mightier and pass away, controls the destinies of nations, shapes the fate of civilizations, balances up from time to time the great accounts between the races and the nations, and rules the outer destinies of men. That mighty Ruling Department is one in which the Occult Hierarchy is ever at work, and there the Ideal Man—the Manu, as he is called in the East, the word being only the word from which our own 'man' is derived, the thinker—is the one who shapes and guides the activities of this Ruling Department, under the Supreme Head of the Hierarchy, the Lord of our world.

And then the Teaching Department, that from which all religions come which inspire and color civilizations: at the head of that department, two grades above the grade of a Master, stands the Supreme Teacher, the Teacher of angels and of men, Whom in the East they call the Wisdom, or Bodhisattva, Whom in the West they call the Christ. His the duty of watching over the spiritual destinies of mankind; of guiding, blessing, maintaining the various religions of the world, founded in outline by Himself. His the duty of appointing one

Master or another as the special Guide and Protector of a special religion, while His own benediction flows ever upon the whole of the living religions of the time. His the great duty of appearing from age to age to inspire a new religion, to strike a keynote, until all the notes shall have been struck that make up the great religious chord of our humanity, varied but all harmonious, giving out different tones but forming one mighty chord.

Looking backwards over the past of our race, we see how He came from time to time, the Bodhisattva of the past, the Christ of the past, Who gave the earlier religions to the great Aryan Race; Who built up the fabric of Hinduism for the Aryan root-stock; Who taught as Thoth in Egypt, later known as Hermes, the mighty Revealer; Who came as Zoroaster to the great Persian Empire, thirty-one thousand years ago; Who came as Orpheus to the Greeks, founding the Orphic Mysteries from which all other Mysteries in Greece were gradually successively derived; Who spoke as the Sun in India, as Light in Egypt, as Fire in Persia, as the exquisite Beauty of Music and Sound in Greece; Who gave to each great nation in turn its own religion, laid in each the foundation of the civilization which that religion was to color and to inspire; and Who, then, having done His work, came forth for the last time in Hindustan, there to reach the Illumination of the Buddha, and with Buddhism closed the ancient cycle, and left to His Successor the opening of the new.

For when the World-Teacher has performed His task, when He has appeared over and over again to build in turn the great religions which it is His function to reveal, then when a great world-age is over, He comes for the last time, speaks His last word, reaches the final Illumination, and passes away from earth. Thus in Buddhism that great cycle of antiquity found its ending; in that great religion the last word of the ancient world was spoken, and He Who had taught, He Who had illuminated, the Christ of that elder world, He passed away, His Work for humanity completed, His task accomplished, His Successor ready to take His place.

Then opened the new cycle, the new age of racial life. The old was closed, the new was to open, and with the fifth sub-race, the Teutonic sub-race that now is leading the nations of the earth, a new cycle was to open, and to it there came the new Bodhisattva, the new Christ, to be the builder of a yet greater civilization. He came among the Jewish people to give out His message and to meet His destiny, to be rejected by His contemporaries, murdered by the people from whom He took His body. But none the less, out of the apparent failure there came a magnificent success; out of the apparent utter breakdown of the mission grew the tree which overshadows Europe and America to-day.

Two notes He struck, both of vital importance, both marking the beginning of a new age, and the line which in due time that age would have to follow.

All the great civilizations of the past had been built on the family as unit. The family, it was declared in India, consists of the man, the wife, and the child. And so if you look back into all those old civilizations, you will see the individual as comparatively nothing, the family the foundation of the State, and out of the families the State built up, and civic duty the mark of highest morality. In the new age the note that was struck was the note of the individual, not of the family, of the value of the individual, of the necessity of the building of the individual, the thought of the one human being standing alone for the time to learn strength and self-reliance. Out of that thought, with all that was necessary for its full evolution, with the clouding of the idea of reincarnation, and the going forward with the loss of that to the idea of an everlasting heaven and an everlasting hell, out of that grew the overwhelming sense of the importance of the present life, of the value of the individual soul, which it was the first duty of Christianity to add to the thought of the world. It meant combat, strife, for a time chaos, well-nigh anarchy, but without that the future would have been impossible. Unless the stone was hewn out of the quarry, unless it was made to be alone for a time, hewn into form, shaped into the necessary appearance, polished; until that was done and the individual stones were ready, a great temple of the Brotherhood of Humanity could not possibly have been builded. Rough is the work of the chisel and the mallet, full of dust and confusion the clamor of the stoneyard; but out of the dust and the clamor, out of the blows and the chipping away, there comes the polished stones of strong individuals fit to be synthesized into a building, fit to be put together to make a mighty Brotherhood; for you must build your Brothers before your Brotherhood can be made. And this past struggle of individualism was a necessary precedent for the building of a mightier and happier race.

And so through all that clash of individualism, through all that chaos of warring classes, men and women see that the Christ breathed another note, lost in the earlier years, but presently to become dominant and all-compelling. It was the teaching that He that is greatest is to be as he that doth serve, that strength accomplished is meant to be yoked to service, that the measure of power is the measure of duty, and that those that are highest should be the helpers of all. Through Christendom the note of self-sacrifice has breathed as it has breathed through none other of the great faiths of earth, and while at first you see the clash of the individuals, you see it is only a means to an end, the fitting of the individual to help. And so out of the teaching of the Christ and the opening of the new cycle there has grown up a civilization battling and tumultuous, but yet in which a social conscience is being born, a realization of human duty, a recognition of human responsibility. And when individualism has done its work, when it has worked out its inevitable destiny, then will come back the Teacher, to show how the stones are to be fitted together; He, the great Master Builder in humanity, He shall again appear, to build up a new sub-race, to shape a universal religion. He literally shall not come to destroy but to fulfil, and to draw around Himself the many creeds of earth; for now the day is approaching when the words He spake shall be fulfilled: "Other sheep I have that are not of this fold; them also I must bring, and they shall hear my voice and shall follow me, and there shall be one fold and one shepherd." And that shepherd shall be the mighty One, Who is the Master of Masters, the Supreme Teacher, the Teacher of the world, Who stands at the head of this Teaching Department of the Occult Hierarchy, Who is the head of all earth's faiths, Who loves and blesses and will unite them all.

But I said there was also a great Ruling Department, in which the Ideal Man stands out as guide. That has also its work going on amongst us, side by side with the gentler, more hidden, more spiritual work of the Christ. Look over the story of man and see how, as you study it, it more and more unfolds the features of a mighty Plan, in which all the races and the sub-races and the nations of mankind have each their appropriate place, each its function and its duty. Look back over history and see the mighty changes that have altered the surface of our globe. Remember how the great naturalists tell us of a time when the huge continent of Lemuria stretched where now the Pacific rolls. See how more and more science is beginning to recognize that once Africa and America could be reached from each other dryshod, and that a vast continent spanned East and West where now is the Atlantic Ocean, and a mighty ruling race was there that spread its civilization far and wide over the globe. See how with our own great Aryan race both these continents have vanished, and the surface of earth and water redistributed makes the habitat for the ruling race of the time. Glance onwards and see the signs of the building again of a coming continent, of islands thrown up in the vast Pacific, of extraordinary volcanic ac-

tivity busy shaping the foundations of a new
continent on which humanity shall live and
flourish, when much of our own has been
broken up, shall have disappeared. Realize
that that changing surface of land and water
goes side by side with the building up of different types of humanity; that the Lemurian
continent had its own type of which the negro
is a mixed remnant to-day; that Atlantis had
also its race, the fourth, of which you can find
traces in the North American Indians, traces
in the old Egyptians, myriads in China and
Japan, for the fourth race is still the most
numerous upon earth. And then see your own
type arising, the great fifth race type, the
Aryan, spreading over the whole of the habi-
table world, divided into its various sub-races,
each distinguishable enough when pure, as
you can distinguish the Kelt from the Teuton,
the Latin from the Scandinavian. See how
that race is spreading and growing, how it is
dominating and ruling, how it is colonizing
and building a mighty Empire. Look onwards
for some hundreds of years, and you will see
that race rising to its summit, building a
mighty World-Empire greater than the past
has known, into which shall flow all the power
and the glory of the nations, in which shall
be incarnate that wondrous group of mighty
intellects, that now and again comes out into
the world to a race when it reaches its zenith,
to be incarnated in the future as in the past in

that wondrous triumph of the great Teutonic sub-race. See how it holds the West, how it is gripping the East; realize that all the spreading has a purpose, and that behind it stands its Manu, guiding and shaping the mighty Empire which yet shall be. Realize that all wars and all conquests have a purpose, that when a nation invades another, over-sweeps it, dominates it for a time, that at that period the nation that is conquered profits, as well as the conqueror who learns his lesson. When the Greeks conquered part of India they brought with them their Art, and left deep imprinted on the Art of India the mark of Greece the all-beautiful. When from Central Asia there swept down into India the mighty flood of the Mughals, that developed another form of Art and enriched the country that they conquered. All these conquests of East by West and West by East work into the mighty Plan, and spread abroad through the nations the treasures that otherwise would be enclosed within the limits of a single country.

Open your eyes to wider horizons; see the mightier, larger Plan; realize that a nation is separated to build up something of value to humanity, and then is spread abroad and scattered that it may carry everywhere that which within its own boundary it made. These wars and conquests, these struggles of nation against nation, of race against race, they all have their place in the mighty Plan; they are guided by the Manu, Who knows exactly what is wanted for each, and makes the wondrous mingling by which humanity grows. Look back, if you will, to the last great struggle that took place in the East between Russia and Japan, and you will see behind those warring armies that two mighty ideals were at grips with each other. Eastern ideals were losing their influence too rapidly; eastern thought was not sufficiently respected. And because the balance which has swung up and down so often between East and West had long been on the side of the West, therefore were East and West flung against each other in those terrible battlefields of Asia, and an eastern nation came out as conqueror for a time, not for itself, but for humanity, that some of the great eastern ideals might not be lost for the world. And so we realize that wherever there is struggle, there the Manu is guiding; that wherever there is turmoil, there the strong hand of the Lord of Men is shaping the future. Oh, it would seem terrible to you if you saw coming down from some vast mountain side, the glacier plowing its way, or the river bursting over all obstacles and spreading flood and destruction in a valley, and blotting out human and animal life. But come back centuries later; visit it again when a thousand years have rolled by, and the same valley plowed by the glacier is glorious with flowers, golden with corn; the children are playing there, and man is happy. Destruction only means rebuilding; death only means new life. Humanity through many trials wins to mightier stature, and the Hierarchy plans and guides for the uplifting of all at last.

And so when over the country to-day there sweeps the storm of unrest and strife, when war of classes—more terrible than war of nations—desolates our country and makes men's hearts tremble with fear; when there seems no outlook; when there seems no remedy; when the resources of the past civilization are exhausted, and those of the future are not yet clearly seen—Oh then remember the words of the Christ: "Let not your heart be troubled," for the birth-pangs of the present have in them the promise of the future. All is well where the Occult Hierarchy, grown from amongst our own flesh and blood made glorious, is behind the warring wills of men, and is shaping even evil to purposes of good.

And so I would leave you with a word not of hope, but of certainty, not of doubt, but of fullest assurance. Where Christ is the Teacher, where the Ideal Man is the Ruler, all must be well with the world of which they are the Lovers and the Guardians. Foundations may break up around us; it is only that they may be better relaid. Buildings may crash down around us; they are outworn, and nobler temples shall arise where they have fallen into ruins. There can be no despair for a race that has produced a Christ and a Buddha. There is no despair for a humanity where men are everywhere growing into God.

WHY WE BELIEVE IN THE COMING OF A WORLD TEACHER [1]

THOSE of you who notice the general statements that we now find scattered about in newspapers, in reports from various countries, in sermons delivered both in the Churches of the Establishment in the south, and by Nonconformist ministers also, may have noticed that there have been recurring references to certain teachings as to the coming of a World Teacher which have been heard from Theosophical platforms, and written about in Theosophical magazines. At first when this was spoken about some years ago, it received but little attention; but, gradually, more and more notice has been taken of it, until now it cannot be said to be confined at all to Theosophical utterances, but a widespread expectation is seen that some great Teacher is likely soon to appear in our world. A few leading men in the Churches have proclaimed their belief in such a coming. From one land after

[1] A lecture delivered in Edinburgh.

another we find the idea coming back to our own, and it seems that those of us who are in some way responsible for bringing the subject before the public have a duty to lay before their fellows some of the reasons which have made them believe in this coming of a Teacher of the world. And I want if I can tonight, to put before you certain lines of thought which suggest that such a belief is rational, to put before you some of the grounds which have led myself and others to think such a coming likely, and in doing this to leave you to judge of the validity of the arguments, of the rationality of the whole conception. At least I will put before you our grounds, and it is for you to judge whether these grounds be solid under our feet or not. Let me remind you at the outset that during the last century, within certain small sections of the Christian community, a good deal was said about what was then called the second coming of the Christ. The idea was fairly familiar about the middle of the last century, though it met more with ridicule than with a wide acceptance. It was put forward along certain traditional lines, and was quite out of accord with the orderly progress of the world. It was supposed that this coming would bring our world to an end. It was thought that the Christ had come once in order to redeem, would return a second time in order to judge, and a considerable number of people—although, indeed, but a minority—considered that the time was coming when the prophecy would find fulfilment. The whole sect of the Irvingites, for instance, held in a very definite way to the idea of the second coming of the Christ. Various bodies scattered through the Churches, affirmed their belief in such a return, and you find still among the Christian communities a very considerable number of people, who hold that idea of the return of the Christ to bring our world completely to an end.

Now, it was pointed out when these statements were made, that if you took the verses that were quoted in the New Testament, and if you looked at them in their original Greek, you did not find there the conception of the end of our world, but rather of the closing of an age or period. The thought that the world had different ages through which it passed had long been familiar in the East, among the Hindus and the Buddhists. It came into the West, and was found among the Greeks and the Romans, and this idea of the winding up of an age, of the closing of a world period, found its way, as has often been pointed out by scholars, into the New Testament, and was connected in these teachings with the return of the Christ.

As the translation became widely spread, and comparatively few concerned themselves about the original statement in the Greek, this idea of the destruction of the world became, as you know, very widely spread in Christendom, but in our own days it found but small acceptance, being, as I said, too much out of accord with the normal line of thinking to make ordinary men of the world, however thoughtful they might be, willing to accept this notion of a sudden conclusion to be put to all the activities of the world in which they were living. And so things remained, until a new view of the relation of great Teachers to the world gradually began to spread among thoughtful people. The conception of World Teachers, as brought forward by the Theosophical Society, developed to a very great extent, although it included the ordinary Christian view of Christ as a great Teacher and Founder of religion.

The Theosophical conception, as widely put forward among thoughtful people, asks them to consider the coming of World Teachers as normal, not as abnormal; as under a certain definite law, and not as a breach of continuity; as part of the Divine plan working out in human evolution, by which these Teachers form a long succession, appearing at quite definite intervals, and accompanied by certain definite signs or conditions in the civilization of the world to which they come. Theosophists, looking back over the world's religions, pointed out that each religion had such a great Teacher as its Founder; that no

matter where you searched in the past, you
found some magnificent figure at the com-
mencement of a new era alike of religion and
civilization; that you could trace a definite
order; that you could recognize a quite intel-
ligible sequence of world religions, rising one
after another and appearing in the world
when the previous civilization and religion
was beginning to show signs of failing in its
power, and of no longer being able thoroughly
to cope with the conditions surrounding it.
That thus, looking back over the long history
of the world, it was possible to see cycles, recurring cycles, each of which began with the
coming of a World Teacher, that coming being followed by a step forward in the evolution of mankind, by the dawning of a new
civilization, embodying some definite prin-
ciple and helping it to evolve along a quite
definite line; that looking thus at the world's
history, one perceived not only that each religion marked a step forward in civilization,
but, also, that it brought out some particular
feature valuable to mankind, on which less
stress had been laid in the religion that pre-
ceded it. And so, gradually there grew up a
conception of religion and civilization which
one may outline briefly in the following way:
that mankind had to learn many lessons and to
develop many different kinds of qualities;
that these lessons and qualities came forward
in special religions which are adapted to em-

phasize particular teachings; that the teachings then were embodied in civilizations; and so humanity, learning the lessons, developing the qualities imparted by the civilizations, gradually shows an advance, with ever enriched qualities, and so, one by one, learns the necessary lessons taught by World Teachers and incorporated in religions. And as you look into the world's history and study it, that view comes out more and more clearly.

Let me just very hastily touch the points of new civilizations and religions, which will give you illustrations of the conception I have just described.

We need not go further back for our purpose than to the beginning of the great Aryan race, from which we all are offshoots. You will find there in its earliest stock, in that stock that developed the great Hindu faith, you find in that Hinduism with its great teacher and ruler, you find certain points coming out definitely and clearly which are the Hindu contribution, as it were, to the great universal religion. You find the idea of the immanence of God; growing out of that the idea of duty; then out of that idea of duty and obligation, there is the recognition of the unity of man. So plainly do these teachings come out and dominate Hinduism, that you find that great missionary, Dr. Millar, one of your own countrymen here, saying, as the result of his many years' work and study, and activity in India, that Hinduism has given to the world two great doctrines, the immanence of God and the solidarity of man.

Pass away from Hinduism, and take the next of the great Teachers and His work. It belongs to what we call the second great migration from the Aryan fatherland. It affects the civilization of Egypt. The name of Thoth —and Hermes, turning the Egyptian name into Greek—is the name of the World Teacher that is there recognized. And His teaching is that of science, which built up the Egyptian religion on profound investigation of Nature and the mastery of natural powers; so that you find the contribution of Egypt to the world's evolution is in the value of science and knowledge of the physical world.

Pass on to the third great migration, that which built up Persia, and you find your world prophet Zoroaster, building up a civilization of which the keynote is purity. "Purity of thought; purity of word; purity of act" —that is the sentence which every Zoroastrian repeats every morning when he rises, and that searching after purity is the mark of the Zoroastrian faith.

Come westwards from Persia into Greece, and you find the great Teacher appearing as Orpheus there. Beauty is the note of the Greek religion and the Greek civilization, and it was the worship, the following of beauty, which made Greece so mighty in the older civilizations of our world.

Come from Greece to Rome, and quite another idea comes out there. There you have the thought of Law—the duty of the citizen to the community. When you take the religion of the Lord Buddha, spread so far and wide in the East, you have the idea of right knowledge, of wisdom, of man learning how to live and seeking in all things to understand.

When you come to Christianity, to that Faith on which has been built the civilization of Christendom, two notes are struck there— the one naturally following upon the other. The first is the value of the individual. You notice in Christianity, as you have never noticed before in the earlier history of religions, that it lays stress on the enormous value of the individual and seeks to build up the idea of individuality; and then, you find in addition to that idea, not so much by precept as by exquisite example, that when power has been gained that power is to be used for service; that when greatness has been attained then the greatest is to be as he that doth serve. And so the notion of self-sacrifice arises, the great contribution of Christianity to the history of religion—that the man realizing himself, knowing himself as an individual, is then to consecrate himself to service, and the measure of his power is to be the measure of his duty.

And so looking on those great Teachers and the religions They gave, you find a quite definite chord sounding out from the whole and every note has its own place, every note its own value; and that view of a succession of World Teachers, instead of the notion of a Teacher having come once for all, only to return as Judge, that wider view of a great sequence of Teachers, and religions, and civilizations, has largely now moulded the thoughts of men, and they begin to realize that what has been, again may be; that as there have been many Teachers in the past, each with His own work and a civilization dependent upon it, therefore there is nothing irrational in the idea that another may be added to that long succession of World Teachers; that another great Teacher may arise Who shall do for the world of our time, what these other Teachers did for the world of Their own day—strike a new note in the great chord of humanity, bring a new inspiration in order that a step forward may once again be taken, give the thought on which shall grow up another civilization; One Who, the lessons of competition having been learned and having made the individual strong, shall teach the lesson of brotherly co-operation and the common good of all as the object each man shall seek; Who shall lay down in some form that idea, which is beginning to show itself here and there amongst us, that there ought to be a minimum of well-being which the organization of society is intended to secure to every one of its children; and that any society that fails to do that is failing in the main object for which it exists: a new departure warranted, first, possibly by the new social conscience which is beginning to develop in our days, and by the coming of a great Teacher Who shall embody, in precept and example, that new conception of man, and make it possible for us, following His precepts, to build up a civilization greater, nobler, more brotherly than the world as yet has ever seen.

And surely there is nothing in that which revolts the common-sense of men. It follows the historical line. It only suggests the recurrence of that which has happened over and over again in the past of our Globe; and once we realize that it is not intrinsically incredible, once we catch the notion that from time to time some great Son of the universal Father comes out to give the younger children a lesson to help in their education, then we naturally turn our thoughts to the next point: Granted that the Teachers come out from time to time, granted that the succession that you suggest is to be traced through history, what is there in the present condition of things that makes you think that we are reaching the ending of one cycle, and the beginning of another? What is there in the condition of the world which in any way justifies you in believing that we have reached the point where another of the long line of Teachers is likely to come forth into the world? That is the next question which seems to demand an answer.

Let me try to put to you the many reasons which render it probable that the world is now standing in one of its transition periods, which mark the passage from one civilization to another, which demands a new departure —because the old seems to have reached the limit of its usefulness, and because along various lines of human activities we see a condition of things is arising which makes it impossible to go further along that line and therefore imperatively demands departure along a new.

One thing that has been noticed in the past with regard to these great changes, is that the surface of our Globe undergoes certain changes in the distribution of land and water, and that these changes coincide with the growth of a new type of human being, from which various sub-types subsequently branch out. May I just interject here the Theosophical idea of human evolution: that we have great race after great race evolving in our world; that each great race has various

branches that we call sub-races; and that
from the sub-race which bears a certain number in sequence, first, second, third, fourth,
fifth, and so on, from the sub-race which
bears that sequential number is chosen out
the next root-race of the same number that is
to appear. That is, that if you are dealing
with the third root-race, the fourth root-race
will be the next that will grow and develop
out of the fourth branch of the preceding third
race. Our own fifth root-race was developed
out of the fifth sub-race of the fourth root-
race. Our next root-race by analogy,
will be developed out of the sixth
sub-race of our present Aryan, or fifth.
Just bear that for a moment in mind, because
then you will realize the force of what I want
to put to you as regards certain physical
things. These great root-races have each a
Continent of its own. You may have read, if
you have studied the great German natural-
ist Haeckel at all, that the human race is said
to have begun on a Continent named Lemuria, which is now sunk below the Pacific,
so that there is water where there was land.
The disappearance of that Continent was accompanied by the rising of another, Atlantis,
and the great fourth race grew and flourished
on that Atlantean Continent, and spread from
it over the whole of the then world. Our own
fifth root-race has for its habitation the land
which you now see in the Continents of our

Globe; the Pacific covering where Lemuria was, the Atlantic covering where once Atlantis flourished.

Now in Hindu books you get the succession —there are certain books called Puranas which give the succession—of the seven Continents on which, it is there said, the seven great races of men either have lived, or will live. They give those that we have already inhabited— that have disappeared; those that now exist; but they tell us of two more, one which is gradually to arise, the dwelling-place of the sixth root-race; another which is to arise for the dwelling-place of the seventh.

There are signs going on in the world in our own time of the rising of a new Continent in the Pacific Ocean. That is not a Theosophical statement but a geological one. And even if you will look at your picture papers, you will have noticed during the last few years pictures from time to time appearing of a new island—one new island after another. These islands which have appeared during the last two or three years are coming up out of what is called the Fiery Ring of the Pacific. That is a great area of earthquake and volcanic activity, and these islands are flung up by volcanic action. They are naturally at present barren, rocky, desolate, flung up in the ocean and remaining there as land. That is going on now, from time to time a new island arising; and geologists tell us that as that goes on a new Continent will arise where now the Pacific Ocean is spreading. They have been asked whether there is danger to the present earth in this arising, and some think that if it comes up very quickly it will be dangerous to all life already on the Globe. From the Theosophical point there is no danger. The thing has happened before and will happen again; and it is so slow and gradual that although there may be local catastrophes and local cataclysms, there is no real danger of world-wide devastation.

Now the beginning of the rising of such a Continent, which takes hundreds of thousands of years in the building, is the first indication of another of these great departures of humanity—another root-race to be born to inhabit that Continent when it is ready for habitation. But as soon as we see signs of such a Continent arising, our minds turn naturally to the question: Well, but what about our fifth race? We have only as yet had five branches of that, and there must be another branch from it before you have the very material out of which the new root-race can gradually develop; so that the mind of the student looks over the earth as it is to-day, looks to see if there is any sign of a new branch of the great fifth root-race; asks whether anywhere there is a new sub-race which is distinguishable from that amid which it is taking its birth?

The answer to that comes from America. The American Bureau of Ethnology has lately received several reports from American ethnologists, and we have there pointed out, definitely and clearly, that a new type of man, different from any now existing, is slowly rendering itself manifest in the United States of America. The measurements of the head and the face are given; the type of the features described—a new sub-race as we call it, a sub-division, as different from the Teuton as the Teuton is different from the Kelt. You can tell at once the difference between the man of pure Latin descent, the Italian and Spaniard, for instance, and the man of the German race—different in build, in color, as well as in mental equipment. You recognize the difference between the definite type of the Teuton and the definite type of the Kelt; and you know that they are as unlike from the standpoint of emotion and mentality as they are unlike in their physical forms. Another such type is now growing up among our American cousins, so clearly differentiated that anyone who goes over to America at intervals of some years will be struck with the increase of this new type, visible to the ordinary observation of anyone who visits the country; so distinct that you recognize it at once as different from the types you know— keenly intellectual, strong-willed, to judge from the cutting of the jaw, but a type entirely distinct, different from the others that we know: so that we who are students of the past, and who from the past are able to some extent, by analogy, to forecast the future, we say that these marks of the new type are showing themselves quite definitely on the other side of the Atlantic Ocean, that the material out of which the great race of the future ages will be evolved is already in the making in America; that that sub-race will increase and multiply; that the type will become more and more dominant, and that, when it has reached, after centuries of evolution, a thoroughly distinctive type and civilization, then there will be the beginning of the other larger growth, of a type to go on for tens of thousands of years before it will be definitely established.

Looking just at these purely physical things, and trying to understand them as signs of the line along which mankind will be evolved, we remember that whenever a new sub-race has appeared a new great Teacher has come to start it on its way. There we find one of the strongest reasons for looking to the coming of the great Teacher within a comparatively short time: that there is in the making a new type, and that always in the past that has been accompanied by the manifestation of a World Teacher. Is it likely, we say, that what has happened over and over again—is it likely that, when looking back

over our own great race, we see how the
Teacher has come with each of these offshoots
that we can trace in the past, that, as we see
the beginning of a new vista when another
type is developing, then the sequence of
Teachers will be broken, and that one type
for the first time will be left unguided, with
none to shape its spiritual aspirations, with
none to lay the foundation of the civilization
that it will be its destiny to build? And we
put that on one side as one of the proofs—a
very important proof when you realize that it
is dealing with physical things that every one
of you can judge about for yourselves.

And we look to see if there are other reasons why we should expect a World Teacher;
and the next thing we notice is that now, as in
the time when the Christ came to the earth,
you are face to face with a great civilization
which has become strong, luxurious, and
dominant, but which is carried on side by side
with an enormous amount of misery and of
wretchedness; which, while on one side it is
undoubtedly magnificent, is on the other side
as undoubtedly miserable, downtrodden, and
depressed. How is our civilization to progress further along the lines on which it is going today? Take the social conditions as you
see them around you now. Look on the terrible unrest in every country in the civilized
world. You cannot take up a newspaper
without seeing in one column after another

references to labor troubles—"The Labor Unrest," "The Strike in Germany," the strike they fear in America, then the strike that is threatened in some other part of the world, to say nothing of the terrible condition over here, where industry is paralyzed, where millions are being driven to the very verge of starvation in the frightful labor war that is desolating our land today. And remember that we had a similar attempt last year, and that after all the trouble then with the railwaymen the supposed arrangement has not even gone on satisfactorily for a single twelvemonth. These recurring troubles, these frightful wars, for they are nothing less than wars, they cannot continue without rending into pieces the body politic. It is impossible to have those convulsions in the labor market without driving thoughtful men to consider the question of new departures, of re-organization, of a change in a system which is palpably breaking down before our eyes. And there is a strange indication, that comes from that American country where our new subrace is arising, of a possibility of an organization of industry, which, though at the moment it be on distinctly anti-social lines, has yet in it the possibility of growing into an organization that would serve society. I mean that flowering of the competitive system into trusts, in which you destroy a large amount of competition, in which one great trade is organized—granted for the benefit of those, a few, who have the control of it—but showing the method in which it might be organized for the benefit of all, and not only of a few; and where we see this system—this wretched deadlock, as I called it some two or three years ago—when we find that industry is going along a road where further progress along the same line is impracticable, then we realize that we are beginning to feel the need of a new organization, of a new type of civilization, and that exactly fits in with the coming of a new sub-race, and demands by all the testimony of the past the coming of a World Teacher.

And it is not only in the labor world that we feel that this deadlock is seen. Along many other lines of human thought and human activity there is the same feeling that we have worn out our old methods and need a new departure in order that progress may be continued. You see it in the world of Art where the old ideals are fading away, and efforts in every direction are being made to body out new forms of art, new conceptions of the beautiful for the growing longings of man. You see it not only in the world of industry and art but in the world of science—the same demand for a new departure because the old methods are beginning to be outworn, and along these lines no further progress seems possible. Endings in every direction! But,

where there are endings there are also beginnings. For the human race has not yet
reached its triumph. Humanity has not completed its mighty evolution. If some things
are fading, it is because others are budding.
If some things are passing away, it is because
new things are coming on. And that great
saying you find in the Christian Scriptures,
"Behold, I create a new Heaven and a new
Earth," that is what rings out from the dying
things of our time; for life is everlasting although forms perish and decay. When we
have seen that so often in the past, we recognize the same signs in the present, we see that
our great civilization—and it is great—is none
the less showing signs of having done its
work. And that we add to our reasons for
looking for a great Teacher; because in the
past these signs have heralded His coming,
therefore, in the present, we regard them as
again but heralding that advent.

And another reason which is stronger than,
perhaps, at first sight you may think, is the
ever-growing expectation and the feeling of
the world that it has need of a teacher. That
took place before the coming of the Christ—a
wide-spread expectation. You see traces of
it in prophecies among many nations, not only
in those of the Hebrew people. You find the
looking for one spread through the Roman
Empire before the Christ appeared—of course
among the Jewish people in their hope of a

Messiah who should conquer, and reign over them. And there is a reason why a widespread expectation should come into the world before some great event appears; for thought always precedes action, and thoughts in the higher worlds are reflected down here as expectations. The thoughts of the great Spiritual Beings Who guide our world, Who shape the fates of nations, Who work out the Divine plan of evolution, and turn the great forces of the earth along channels which are deliberately made in order that they may flow in them and so bring about new conditions in our earth, the thoughts of these mighty Beings turn to the changing times full of the knowledge that a great Teacher is coming, for They are engaged in the preparation for that coming in the superphysical world. The whole of these great thought forms, as we call them, are flung down into the atmosphere of our earth, and create in the minds of men a widespread expectation, which is then but a promise of swift realization. That proverb, "Coming events cast their shadows before," really bodies a truth; for events exist in the world of mind before they exist in the world of matter. Thoughts come before activities, and a thought, the shadow of the event, is a prophecy of the coming event. And so wherever you find a very wide-spread expectation you may be sure that there is a reality in the higher world of which that expectation is the shadow. That wide-spread expectation which now is spreading among the great religions of the world, in all the great religious organizations of the world, is literally a prophecy of the event which is to crown these expectations with realization, the thought-heralds of the coming Teacher preparing His way before Him.

But it is not only the world's expectation; it is the world's need. That view, perchance, will appeal only to those who believe that the world is guided, helped, protected by higher powers than humanity, by mightier Beings than ourselves; Who look on the world as the huge field of evolution in which Spirits are unfolding, and which exists for the very purpose of their unfoldment; Who realize that the world has a mighty Architect Who plans out the progress of humanity, and that that plan is worked out stage by stage by His agents, His subordinates, who build slowly along the lines of the plan that He has designed and conceived. Then all those, when they see the terrible need of the world of to-day, feel that they need some Master to voice and to bring down the help of which the world feels the sore necessity. And those social problems to which I alluded mark out the need of our world. We need a leader, one greater than ourselves, who, seeing these mighty problems that to us are insoluble, will point us to the road along which we may walk to their solu-

tion, one who will apply to the tangle of earthly life these fundamental truths of morality
which are unchanging and eternal, but which
have never yet been thoroughly applied to
human society, or to the organizing of men on
the principles there laid down.   The great
Teachers have all spoken with one voice.
They have told us: "Love one another." They
have told us that hate ceases not by hatred
at any time, that hatred ceases but by love;
but although that was taught by the Lord
Buddha twenty-five centuries ago, although
the Christ in His exquisite Sermon on the
Mount pressed that same eternal teaching in
words familiar to you all, where do we find
one nation that puts these principles into
practice, where is a single organization
which is built according to that moral law?
There is the great need, then, of our time. We
know the principles; but we know not how to
apply them.   We realize that love should be
the foundation of our Social Union; but we
know it is not, that rivalry, and competition, and struggle are the principles on which
our Society is builded up; and we need some-
one who will speak to us with an authority
which appeals at once to our hearts and our
brains, and lead us along that better road of
Brotherhood which has been taught for ages
but never practiced, which is realized as a
duty in the family, but not realized as equally
a duty in the State.   We need a new inspira-

tion which will make us willing to work along these lines, and inspire us with the faith which will enable us to overcome the difficulties in our road, and venture to apply these principles to the guidance of nations as well as of individuals.

I grant that there are many individuals in every nation now who are trying to mould their lives by these eternal precepts; but there is not one nation that appears to put them into practice, that does not, while pretending to believe them, give them the lie by every arrangement that they make for defence of themselves and attack of their brother nations, which does not, in every class division, negate the principles that they acknowledge with their lips. And so we need a great Teacher, not so much to give us new truth, as to give us the inspiration which will enable us to make the old truths the practical guide of our lives; and when He comes to teach and to inspire, we shall not expect that He will do it all for us, and so deprive us of the value of the training and the learning, but rather that He shall point the way, and lead us in the way, so that we may gradually learn to solve our problems for ourselves in the light that shall come forth from Him. For humanity has grown since last He was here. Humanity has developed since last a World Teacher trod our earth. The minds of men have grown. The mental average of man is

higher than it has been before. A social conscience is growing; a social conscience is beginning to develop; and we no longer look for
a great One Who shall come as a conqueror to
lift us into power, but for a Teacher Who shall
guide us into truth, and Who shall enable us
to make our actions commensurate with our
aspirations.

There has come to our world a dream of social life which has dazzled the eyes of many,
has warmed the hearts of all. You can see
spreading over our country among the highly
educated and the wealthy, a new sense of
responsibility, a new desire of service, a discontent with the luxury which they have, but
others do not share, a longing to sacrifice
themselves in order that others may profit by
the sacrifice. Among our young men and our
young women that spirit is showing itself
more and more, as the boys and the girls
grow up into young manhood and young
womanhood. It is not the old amongst us,
now fossilized into indifference, who will build
the Kingdom of the coming Christ, and make
a new civilization based on love and on
brotherhood. His appeal will be to the young,
whose hearts are warm, whose brains are
keen, who feel the longing to labor, to love,
and to sacrifice, thousands of young men and
young women growing up to-day, who are
longing to give themselves to human service
and only asking: "What can we do in order

that the world may be the better for our living?" And in that feeling so widely spread, in that passionate enthusiasm which is moving the present generation of the younger amongst us, in that I see the growing body of disciples who will surround the Christ when He comes to teach, and will be led by Him to the realization of a nobler social order. That is the true preparation for His coming; that is the real sign that He will soon be among us. Those who are willing to work, those who are willing to toil, those who are willing to sacrifice, they shall be the peaceful army that He shall lead to the conquest of the great ideal Society, which they shall build under His direction and make practicable under His inspiration; and they, perhaps more than any other proof, are the sign of the new departure, are the welcome and the heralds of the coming Teacher.

And if, friends, looking over the line of thought that I have traversed hastily to-night, if glancing back to the history of the past, you are able to see there something of the promise of the future; if you realize something of the changing world around you, the physical earth showing signs of alteration; if you see the beginnings of the new type, of the new sub-race; if you understand something of the problems around us and the hopelessness of trying to solve them along lines previously used; if you realize the growing expectation, the looking for the coming of One to lead and to guide, and then you realize that while He is preparing for His coming, His children are preparing to welcome Him and are getting ready to march under His banner and to carry out His will; then I think that to you, as well as to some of us, there will rise up the hope, nay, the certainty, that we are on the eve of mighty changes to be carried out under a World Teacher, Who shall come to our help, Who shall act as our Guide; and as that thought grows strong in your hearts, life will grow full of hope, full of joyful expectation. You will realize that the world is not left alone, that the troubles of the present are but the birth-pangs out of which a new civilization shall be born; and that just as in the coming of a longed-for son the pain is forgotten in the joy of welcome, so, the troubles of our time, menacing and terrible as they are, are but that hour that precedes the dawning, are but the sufferings that precede the birth; and that we also shall ere very, very long realize that change is upon us, that the Teacher is with us, that hope has changed into realization, and that the longing for the coming has altered into the delight of the come.

A SELECTED LIST OF
THEOSOPHICAL BOOKS

❈

PRICE
The Riddle of Life. Annie Besant	$ .25
The Life After Death. C. W. Leadbeater	.25
An Outline of Theosophy. C. W. Leadbeater	.60
Popular Lectures on Theosophy. Annie Besant	.75
A Textbook on Theosophy. C. W. Leadbeater	1.00
At the Feet of the Master. J. Krishnamurti	.60
Hints to Young Students of Occultism. L. W. Rogers	.75
Theosophy and the New Psychology. Annie Besant	1.00
Dreams. C. W. Leadbeater	.60
Clairvoyance. C. W. Leadbeater	.85
Invisible Helpers. C. W. Leadbeater	1.00
Some Glimpses of Occultism. C. W. Leadbeater	2.25
Man Visible and Invisible. C. W. Leadbeater	4.50
Thought Forms. Annie Besant and C. W. Leadbeater	4.50
The Inner Life. C. W. Leadbeater. (New American edition of 749 pages in one volume)	4.75
Man and His Bodies. Annie Besant	.60
The Changing World. Annie Besant	1.75
The Immediate Future. Annie Besant	1.00
The Ideals of Theosophy. Annie Besant	.85
In the Outer Court. Annie Besant	1.00
The Path of Discipleship. Annie Besant	1.00
Esoteric Christianity. Annie Besant	1.75
The Ancient Wisdom. Annie Besant	1.75

CATALOG ON REQUEST
THE THEOSOPHICAL PRESS
826 Oakdale Avenue
Chicago

CPSIA information can be obtained
at www.ICGtesting.com
Printed in the USA
BVHW052228171218
535769BV00016B/1052/P